when harlem
nearly killed king

when harlem nearly killed king

THE 1958 STABBING OF DR. MARTIN LUTHER KING, JR.

Hugh Pearson

SEVEN STORIES PRESS

New York ~ London ~ Toronto ~ Sydney

SEVEN STORIES PRESS
140 Watts Street
New York, NY 10013
http://www.sevenstories.com

IN CANADA: Hushion House, 36 Northline Road, Toronto, Ontario M4B 3E2

IN THE U.K.: Turnaround Publisher Services Ltd., Unit 3, Olympia Trading Estate, Coburg Road, Wood Green, London N22 6TZ

IN AUSTRALIA: Tower Books, 2/17 Rodborough Road, Frenchs Forest NSW 2086

Library of Congress Cataloging-in-Publication Data

Pearson, Hugh
When Harlem nearly killed King : the 1958 stabbing of Martin Luther King, Jr. / Hugh Pearson.
p. cm.
ISBN 1-58322-274-X
1. King, Martin Luther, Jr., 1929-1968—Assassination attempt, 1958. 2. Attempted murder—New York (State)—New York—History—20th century. 3. Harlem (New York, N.Y.)—History—20th century. 4. Harlem (New York, N.Y.)—Race relations. 5. New York (N.Y.)—History—1951–6. New York (N.Y.)—Race relations. 7. Stab wounds—Treatment—New York (State)—New York—History—20th century. 8. Harlem Hospital Center—History. I. Title.
E185.97.K5 P42 2002
364.15'24'092—dc21
2001007352
9 8 7 6 5 4 3 2 1

College professors may order examination copies of Seven Stories Press titles for a free six-month trial period. To order, visit www.sevenstories.com/textbook, or fax on school letterhead to (212) 226-1411.

Book design by POLLEN

Printed in the U.S.A.

CONTENTS

where do we go from here?

EUPHORIA FROM THE November 13, 1956, Supreme Court decision desegregating buses in Montgomery, Alabama, after a year-long boycott spread across the country. It deluged soon to be twenty-eight-year-old Reverend Martin Luther King, Jr., with speaking engagements, requests for advice on how to organize similar boy-cotts in other Southern cities and towns, and suggestions of new local Jim Crow targets for the Montgomery Improvement Association (MIA), the organization that had spearheaded the boy-cott. A year earlier, King had been the city's new Negro pastor, treated by most of the established Negro leaders of Montgomery as gullible enough to take the heat for boldly trying to convince ordi-nary Negroes who depended on the mass transit system in the small capital city to stay away and instead walk or carpool to work until their demands were met—a risky proposition that most observers initially predicted would end in disaster. The middle-class and well-to-do Negroes of Montgomery, especially the leaders of the most influential churches (who never rode the buses anyway) concluded that King could afford to take a foolish risk because he was new enough and young enough (thus naïve enough) not to accommodate the city's Caucasian power structure. He had no relationships that could be jeopardized or doomed.

Then, after pulling off the miracle, due to the gravity of the achievement it became impossible for King to return to a normal life. The boycott soon ended up enlisting the aid of even the initial doubters, who didn't want to be judged too harshly by posterity. In the aftermath of victory, King would garner the lion's share of strokes to the ego, as well as the attendant pressures and dangers that came along with becoming an icon. Part of him wanted to return to something resembling a normal life. But now that was impossible.

During the year in which the protesters held out for the victory, King led them across a moral and philosophical watershed. Near the beginning of the boycott, the Caucasian power structure of Montgomery lost patience with a unity enabling them to organize as many as 350 automobiles for carpools. After two months of this, city officials decided to search through the municipal ordinances to find some way to rein in the protest, only to discover a 1921 statute prohibiting boycotts "without just cause or legal excuse." At that point they convened a grand jury, which soon returned indictments against the boycott leaders, meaning, of course, that all of them were to be arrested and stand trial (but would be released on bail). Up until then, the thinking among decent, respectable Negro citizens had been, It was one thing to stay off of buses (or anywhere else you were allowed) voluntarily, but quite another to be arrested, and possibly convicted for doing so, ending up with a criminal record. Did they really want to besmirch their reputations and possibly compromise their futures in such a manner?

King was out of town when the indictments were handed out. On his way back to Montgomery through his hometown of Atlanta, he was met by his nervous father (known as Daddy King) who was certain that this was a line his son should not cross. The elder King convened a group of friends, the most prominent Negroes in Atlanta (including the president of King's alma mater, Morehouse College) to come by his home and help him convince King junior not to return to Montgomery. But the younger King was adamant that he be arrested with the other leaders. Upon hearing this, King senior cried like a baby.

Daddy King sensed the greater implications of what was happening, as did others. At first he predicted disaster for the boycott effort and the possible murder of his son. The entire nation watched in amazement as the determination of the city's Negro citizens remained high. Elsewhere in the South there had been isolated protests of segregation ordinances. But such protests fizzled. None of them lasted this length of time, or featured unity and resolve in such large numbers. Among those captivated by what was taking place was Bayard Rustin, a forty-six-year-old New York City–based itinerant activist with pacifist sensibilities. Rustin headed for Montgomery just as the boycott leaders were about to be arrested. With his Gandhian sensibilities, he was destined to become a key aide to King. The first advice he offered was that the boycott leaders not wait for police officers to come and arrest them as if they were common criminals. Rather, they should seize the moral high ground and appear at jail to give themselves up. Their proactive gesture had the effect of shocking the law enforcement officers. As word spread of what they were doing, spectators showed up to cheer them on. The tactic further backfired on the city when the indictments prompted the legal process that eventually led the Supreme Court to outlaw segregation on Montgomery buses.

While he did his best to handle the attention and demands that cascaded upon him due to the boycott's success, King was introduced to another man who would become very important in defining the direction of future activism. Stanley Levison was a forty-four-year-old independently wealthy New York City–based socialist (his fortune due to wise real estate investments) with a passionate concern for what was taking place in the Deep South. After the 1955 lynching of Emmett Till in Mississippi (the fifteen-year-old who had allegedly wolf-whistled at a Caucasian woman), Levison, who was Jewish, helped launch an emergency organization called In Friendship, to raise money in the North for victims of Southern racial violence. As the Montgomery bus boycott dragged on, In Friendship also raised money to support the boycotters. Up until Rustin introduced him to King, this had been the extent of Levison's involvement as a facilitator of change in the South.

Boycotting Montgomery's buses had been relatively easy compared with the other arenas in which Jim Crow existed. Municipal transit systems depended on Negro as well as Caucasian patronage. However, to eradicate the practice among other municipal facilities (to say nothing of privately owned establishments) would require a far more brazen confrontation with Southern authority. Would the protesters go to jail (and suffer even worse consequences) for being somewhere Jim Crow did not allow them? It was far easier for King to accept the constant invitations from across the country to *preach* against the evils of segregation than it was to deal with this conundrum. In the aftermath of the Montgomery victory, he was making as many as four speeches per week (which would work out to approximately two hundred per year), and his powerful oratory was bringing audiences to their feet.

With these difficulties in mind, Levison's first idea for what the movement should do next was for King to broadcast his own regularly scheduled national television or radio program designed to persuade the nation to stop the practice of segregation. All that was needed was a corporate sponsor. In 1957 this was not a realistic possibility. No major company was about to take such a risk.

Other ideas included tackling segregation city by city, town by town, by holding racially mixed mass meetings in which King would communicate the ideals that formed the basis of the bus boycott, first in the North, then in border states, then in the Deep South. Such a tactic would amount to crusades against segregation modeled off of the religious crusades of evangelist Billy Graham.

In fact, at one point King discussed holding such rallies in tandem with Graham. But the idea foundered on the issue of where the greater stress should be placed—political change or religious transformation. Graham was a moderate and thus believed he couldn't get too political. He felt he had to walk a fine line so as not to turn off his Caucasian religious supporters. Eventually the crusade idea was modified (Graham had nothing to do with this modification). Instead of pushing for citizens of all persuasions to agitate for desegregation, the Southern Leadership Conference (SCLC)—the new organization King had founded in the aftermath of the Montgomery victory to further civil rights interests across the South—would launch crusades in Southern cities and towns to register Negro citizens to vote. The campaign would be called the Crusade for Citizenship. Yet it, too, would meet with disappointment, as the turnout in places where King was to speak ended up being quite small, and the number of new voters registered, negligible. It appeared that the level of excitement about what the boycott had accomplished still outweighed the risks Negroes in the South were willing to take to abolish discrimination on the next level.

As he tried to figure out what to do next, King also had problems with the leadership of his own religious denomination. After the Montgomery victory, he dreamed of turning the five-million-member National Baptist Convention into a civil rights vehicle by electing a president allied to his interests. The twenty thousand ministers and their congregations for his cause would be a far more potent force to count on than the hundred or so ministers and congregations who formed SCLC. It would also be far more powerful than the NAACP. But this idea, too, would come to nothing after J. H. Jackson, current president of the Baptist convention, who was not about to be upstaged by King, got his cronies to vote by acclamation to reelect him president in violation of the Baptist convention's own constitution. Over the years Jackson would consolidate his power and block the denomination from ever formally supporting the civil rights movement.

In the months following the boycott victory, reporters began alleging there were other Negro leaders who were jealous of King. This was an understandable sentiment in light of the manner in which King had rocketed to fame virtually overnight, while so many of them had spent entire careers agitating for civil rights through other channels or otherwise distinguishing themselves. Just a few months after the boycott victory, several American Negro leaders were aboard an airplane heading to the newly formed nation of Ghana, formerly the West African colony known as the Gold Coast, to celebrate its independence. They included Nobel Peace Prize–winner Ralph Bunche (who won the award in 1950 for his role in helping quell the ongoing Arab-Israeli conflict); Congressman Adam Clayton Powell, Jr., of New York, the most powerful Negro politician in the nation; Mordecai Johnson, president of Howard University, the largest Negro university in the country; A. Phillip Randolph, head of the first labor union to organize Negroes and the man responsible for forcing President Franklin Roosevelt to issue an executive order during World War II ensuring Negro employment in wartime industry, the same man who founded the Brotherhood of Sleeping Car Porters; and Martin Luther King, Jr., recent subject of a cover story in *Time* magazine, due to the Montgomery victory. Of the five leaders only King was invited into the cockpit by the plane's crew and provided the honorary opportunity of playfully taking the controls.

The following May saw King organize a Prayer Pilgrimage to Washington, D.C., in light of the refusal of President Eisenhower to even listen to Negro grievances at that point. But it took the NAACP working its back channels with the presidential administration to get approval of the Lincoln Memorial as the staging area. While privately consulting with White House aides, the lawyer who successfully argued before the Supreme Court *Brown v. The Board of Education of Topeka, Kansas*, which outlawed school segregation, and future Supreme Court justice himself, Thurgood Marshall, repeatedly referred to King as a "first-rate rabble-rouser," assuring Maxwell Raab, the White House's designated point man on "Negro issues," that in exchange for the go-ahead the NAACP would make sure that King's emotional pulpit style was toned down. With this assurance clearance was received. And the reception given to King at the Pilgrimage prompted the media to further single him out as the titular Negro leader.

While King continued to try to figure out the best direction in which to take the movement, Levison had settled on at least one way he could capitalize on the nationwide interest generated up to that point: write a book describing how tired maids, washwomen, manual laborers, cooks, gardeners, nannies, and chauffeurs had been inspired to stay off of Montgomery buses until the Supreme

Court ruled in their favor. Using his connections in publishing, Levison persuaded Harper and Brothers to sign King to write what was to be called *Stride Toward Freedom: The Montgomery Story* for an advance against royalties of $3,500.

The goal the editors set for King's book was to explain the movement to Caucasians. It was to be intellectual, but not too dry. Neither should it come across as "too Negro." It was designed to promote King as "a leader of his people," but also to steer clear of anything that could be interpreted as favorable to Communism. *Stride Toward Freedom* would become the first book about a major civil rights event, yet not a vital manifesto in the pantheon of books written on the era, since it was penned at the dawn of the movement.

Though he now had a book contract in hand, King found it difficult to pull himself away from his constant speaking engagements. This caused him to fall behind on the deadline Harper editors had set for receiving the finished manuscript. They were convinced there was a finite window of opportunity for telling the story, after which few Caucasians would be interested. "To prepare and preach sermons is to use up creative energy that your soul and body wants to use on this book," wrote one editor in a follow-up letter after flying down to Montgomery to meet with King. King continued preaching. Finally, the Harper editors ordered him to spend $2,000 of his $3,500 advance to pay one of their staffers, Hermine Popper, to coordinate the project, seeing to it that drafts of the book's chapters circulate between her, King, Levison, Rustin, another adviser named Harris Wofford, and the designated historian for the MIA, L. D. Reddick.

Among the five, Levison served as King's harshest critic, doing his best to steer him clear of anything that could be interpreted as egocentric. From his perch in New York City, Levison told King that the manuscript needed more about the movement itself, more about the roles of other key players in the drama. He told King that the one chapter it didn't need was the one he had written about "Negro self-improvement." Calling for a change in character among Negroes, Levison felt, was out of the question. Never mind that the basis for much of what they were fighting was Caucasian belief in Negro licentiousness, ignorance, and laziness, that in King's opinion there needed to be a simultaneous attack on these canker sores roosting on the integrity of Negroes as a whole. To Levison, all of that had to be glossed over in favor of maintaining the momentum the boycott victory had generated.

King accepted most of the advice, limiting his criticisms of Negroes as a whole to a few paragraphs in the last chapter of the book. The book began with what had brought him to Montgomery:

> The previous August of 1953, after being in school for twenty-one years without a break, I had reached the satisfying moment of completing the residential requirements for my Ph.D. degree [at Crozier Theological Seminary]. The major job that remained was to write my doctoral thesis. In the meantime I thought it would be wise to start considering a job so that I could be placed by September 1954. Two churches in the East—one in Massachusetts and one in New York—had expressed interest in calling me. Three colleges had offered me attractive and challenging posts—one a teaching post, one a deanship, and the other

an administrative position. In the midst of thinking about all of
these positions, I received a letter from the officers of the Dexter
Avenue Baptist Church of Montgomery, saying that they were
without a pastor and that they would be glad to have me preach [on
a trial basis] when I was again in that section of the country.

Then it detailed how Rosa Parks had been arrested on
December 1, 1955, for refusing to give up her seat to a Caucasian,
and how the idea to boycott the buses as a result of her arrest originated with a pullman porter named E. D. Nixon (in later accounts,
a group of middle-class Negro women would be credited with sug-
gesting the idea to Nixon, who allegedly told them that he was
thinking along the same lines):

> Early Friday morning, December 2, Nixon called me. He was so
> caught up in what he had to say that he forgot to greet me with
> the usual "hello" but plunged immediately into the story of what
> had happened to Mrs. Parks the night before. I listened, deeply
> shocked, as he described the humiliating incident. "We have
> taken this type of thing too long already," Nixon concluded, his
> voice trembling. "I feel the time has come to boycott the buses.
> Only through a boycott can we make it clear to the white folks
> that we will not accept this type of treatment any longer."

King's book described how the following week, the Montgomery
Improvement Association was formed and King was voted president. Then, later in the book, King described how the Dexter Avenue
parsonage was bombed during the boycott:

> On January 30 [1956], I left home a little before seven to
> attend our Monday evening mass meeting at the First Baptist

Church. A member of my congregation, Mrs. Mary Lucy Williams, had come to the parsonage to keep my wife company during my absence. After putting the baby [Yolanda] to bed, Coretta and Mrs. Williams went to the living room to look at television. About nine-thirty they heard a noise in front that sounded as though someone had thrown a brick. In a matter of seconds an explosion rocked the house. A bomb had gone off on the porch.

No one was injured in the blast, and the boycott continued. Yet King detailed his fears that when the mass arrests began three weeks later, the boycott, indeed, would come to an end:

> All night long I thought of the people of Montgomery. Would these mass arrests so frighten them that they would urge us to call off the protest? I knew how hard-pressed they had been. For more than thirteen weeks they had walked, and sacrificed, and worn down their cars. They had been harassed and intimidated on every hand. And now they faced arrest on top of all of this. Would they become battle-weary, I wondered. Would they give up in despair? Would this be the end of the movement?"

He ended the book with a forecast of what would come next:

> It is becoming clear that the Negro is in for a season of suffering. As victories for civil rights mount in the federal courts, angry passions and deep prejudices are further aroused. . . . State laws continue to be enacted to circumvent integration. I pray that, recognizing the necessity of suffering, the Negro will make of it a virtue. To suffer in a righteous

cause is to grow in our humanity's stature. If only to save himself from bitterness, the Negro needs the vision to see the ordeals of this generation as the opportunity to trans-figure himself and American society. If he has to go to jail for the cause of freedom, let him enter it in the fashion that Gandhi urged his countrymen, 'as the bridegroom enters the bride's chamber'—that is, with a little trepidation but with great expectation.

Levison and Rustin polished these passages to a sheen (but asked that their names be left out of the book's acknowledgments due to their controversial status as alleged "Communist agitators"). And within nine months the manuscript was ready. Harper and Brothers scheduled publication for September 17, 1958.

Now the challenge was, how to kick off the publicity campaign for the book. The answer: Bring King to New York City to appear on national TV. All King had to do was show up in the section of Manhattan famous for developing or showcasing national Negro leaders. For this occasion his most prominent rivals would feel compelled to muzzle their jealousies. They would feel obligated to publicly support all that King represented because they were eager to bask in his glory, anxious to capitalize on his appearances in Harlem churches, bookstores, a department store, and at a sched-uled political rally. What King didn't know at the time was that upon heading to New York City, he personally would experience his own ordeal, testing the metal and strength that he suggested at the end of his book Negroes would need in the future. And the person who instigated this crisis wouldn't be any of the VIPs eager for photo opportunities with him. It wouldn't be an assassin hired by angry racists. The person he should have been warned against on his trip to New York City was someone else altogether, the last individual anyone would have dreamed had anything against Martin Luther King, Jr.

a tight race

BY SEPTEMBER 1958, New York governor W. Averell Harriman, scion of one of the most prominent and wealthy families in the nation, was locked in a tight gubernatorial battle with another scion of wealth—the charismatic, womanizing grandson of the most feared, reviled, and wealthy pioneer of America's Gilded Age. His opponent's grandfather, John D. Rockefeller, Sr., had virtually single-handedly caused lawmakers in Washington, D.C., to pass the nation's antitrust laws, forcing the breakup of his Standard Oil Trust, a behemoth that controlled the sale of 90 percent of the nation's oil. But by the time they got around to doing so, it was already too late to prevent Rockefeller from amassing the largest personal fortune of any man on earth.

At age sixteen, patriarch John D. Rockefeller, Sr., took a job as a bookkeeper. By the age of thirty-one, with three partners he founded his oil company, eventually buying them out and parlaying his net worth to close to a billion dollars. At the age of fifty-seven, he created the Rockefeller Foundation, the world's largest philanthropic organization, and through it, gave away $530 million, setting up his only son, John junior, and family to create a reputation of family beneficence that would gloss over all he had done to amass the fortune and assuage any feelings of guilt they might have. Of the six children John junior and his wife had, five were boys. And of those five, all but Nelson and Winthrop would do their best to stay out of the limelight and quietly lead lives of discreet wealth and charity (reluctantly tolerating the exposure of the family caused by the political ambitions of their two brothers).

It was Nelson who challenged Harriman in 1958 for the governorship of New York. Extremely extroverted, he combined a hunger for womanizing with a hunger to climb whatever career mountains he wanted to, in the most public of manners. In September 1958, at the age of fifty, Nelson felt qualified to challenge Harriman because his record of philanthropic and appointive positions was an impressive one. In the midst of the Great Depression he had presided over the creation and construction of Rockefeller Center, that collection of majestic skyscrapers in midtown Manhattan, replete with a golden Zeus presiding over an open-air plaza. After that he had involved himself in a vast array of public initiatives, and had been appointed to a variety of posts by U.S. presidents. Nelson had helped found the Albert Einstein School of Medicine in the Bronx section of New York City. He helped cajole Congress into earmarking six million dollars in new construction for predominantly Negro Howard University, presided over by the same Mordecai Johnson who flew with King to the new nation of Ghana. He had directed the revitalization of Gallaudet College in Washington, D.C., the world's only college for the deaf and training center for teachers of the deaf. He had engaged in an array of do-good projects in Latin America (to make up for the capitalist machinations fostered by his family's economic interests in that region), bringing supermarkets, mechanized farming, and low-cost housing to Puerto Rico, Brazil, Peru, El Salvador, and Guatemala. He was chosen assistant Secretary of State for Latin American Affairs by President Roosevelt, and coordinated Inter-American Affairs during World War II; was assigned to the founding conference of the United Nations by President Truman; then was chosen by the next president, Dwight Eisenhower, as Undersecretary of Health, Education and Welfare. Besides his support for Howard University, Nelson consistently donated to the National Urban League and other human rights organizations. And he could boast that Spelman College, perhaps the finest college in the nation for Negro women, was endowed with his family's wealth and named after his paternal grandmother, Laura Spelman Rockefeller.

The record of his opponent, the incumbent governor, was impressive as well. And Harriman had the implied benefit of maturity (at the age of sixty-six he was sixteen years Nelson's senior) as well as incumbency in elective (rather than appointive office) on his side. The founder of the fortune Averell lived off of hadn't been his grandfather. Rather, it had been his father. Edward H. Harriman (known as E. H.) had been a shrewd, hated, and feared railroad industry manipulator. Born in 1848 the son of an Episcopalian preacher and raised on Long Island, he quit school at fourteen and, by the age of twenty-two, founded his own Wall Street brokerage firm. Nine years later he married a woman whose father owned a small railroad, and from there the rest, as they say, was history. E. H. Harriman shrewdly took control of the Illinois Central Railroad, bought the bankrupt Union Pacific Railroad, squared off with J. P. Morgan for control of Northern Pacific Railroad, fighting him to a draw. By the time he died in 1909, E. H. Harriman left his family with a $100 million fortune. Averell was just seventeen years old.

With wealth to cushion him, the tall, handsome Averell was educated at Yale. After graduation he presided over the family business interests. Then, foreseeing a worldwide depression, in 1928 he voted for Democrat Al Smith for president (who, of course, would lose to Republican Herbert Hoover). Soon thereafter, he effectively left the business world. During the Great Depression, President Roosevelt appointed Harriman to the National Relief Administration (NRA). With the coming of World War II, he served as Roosevelt's envoy to England prior to American entry into the war. From there he would be appointed by Roosevelt and then Truman to a succession of posts: director of the lend-lease program to England; ambassador to Russia and

England; a field captain of the Marshall Plan; director of the Mutual Security Administration. Then in 1954, he decided to take the plunge into elective politics by running for governor of New York. He won the general election contest against Republican opponent Irving Ives by a mere 11,625 votes and began establishing the record with which he'd run for reelection four years later against Nelson Rockefeller.

That record included accomplishments designed to placate upstate New York at the expense of the New York City metropolitan area, causing the growth of animus for Harriman among New York City Democrats. To the consternation of Tammany Hall, Harriman built roads and schools for upstaters and developed resorts in the Adirondacks. Yet he also instituted benefits that all New Yorkers could enjoy, increasing overall state aid for education by 78 percent; increasing benefits for the unemployed and those disabled on the job; increasing the minimum wage. In essence, in 1958, both parties had put up for governor opponents who balanced each other out by appealing to constituencies their parties traditionally didn't appeal to, and who harbored so much family wealth that no one could accuse them of engaging in graft while in office. Yet as the gubernatorial race entered its final months, Harriman also had to put out a major internal party brushfire.

As a result of what he had done for upstate New York, and because of his aloof, patrician bearing, Harriman was forced to compete with legendary New York City Tammany Hall boss Carmine De Sapio for control of the state party. And the manner in which they squared off revolved around the tug-of-war over who would be the party's nominee that year for U.S. senator. Initially, De Sapio's faction wanted New York City Mayor Robert Wagner. But Harriman, with an eye toward the future, had no intention of backing Wagner because he viewed him as a potential rival for a slot in a Democratic presidential administration should the party prevail in 1960. After Harriman turned down Wagner, De Sapio's faction backed Manhattan district attorney Frank Hogan. But the liberal faction of the party didn't want Hogan. Thus the *battle royale* commenced. Harriman sifted through a variety of possibilities, circling back to New York City Mayor Robert Wagner. But Wagner, angry at the initial rebuff, turned Harriman down. And with no decent alternative, Hogan won the nomination, registering a symbolic "rat fuck," (in the words of Harriman's mince-no-words wife), of Harriman on the part of De Sapio, after which the Democratic Party had to heal itself going into the election's final stretch, in order to rebuff the Rockefeller challenge to the governor.

The strategy on the part of the Republicans was to paint Harriman as not in control of his own party, while that of the Democrats was to try to paint Rockefeller as beholden, when push came to shove, to traditional Republican interests and values. Both candidates had to secure their bases while appealing to enough undecided voters to win the election. And no constituency was more up for grabs than Afro-American voters. In 1958, the nation's civil rights agenda was front and center in the news. Besides the 1954 *Brown v. the Board of Education* decision outlaw-

ing school segregation and the 1956 Montgomery Bus Boycott victory, the previous fall there had been the school desegregation
battle in Little Rock, Arkansas, which had captivated the nation.
A year later it was still holding everyone in thrall, because
Arkansas governor Orvall Faubus closed the state's public schools
rather than obey the Supreme Court's order to integrate them.
Elected officials everywhere were taking stands. In the South, support for Faubus became the litmus test of loyalty to "traditional
Southern values," while among politicians in large Northern
urban areas, opposition to what Faubus stood for became the litmus test for whether or not traditional liberals were up-to datc on
the latest position liberals were supposed to take on the race issue.
On this subject, both Harriman and Rockefeller could afford to
embrace liberalism.

The worried Harriman, for instance, blanketed Negro communities with campaign pamphlets showing him and his wife
with Little Rock school desegregation leader Daisy Bates as she
visited the couple in the governor's mansion. The text detailed
his list of accomplishments, including hiring Negroes to two state
judicial posts: State Rent Administrator and Assistant Counsel to
the Governor, as well as to other posts. It reminded Negro voters
that Harriman had launched fair employment and fair housing
initiatives, and that he had spoken out against school segregation in Little Rock. In that same literature—well aware that, as an
individual, Rockefeller had spoken out against segregation too—
Harriman and his aides attempted to bypass the man himself in
leveling their criticism and going after the rest of his party with

statements like: "Republican officials have been counseling Negroes to be patient [on the subject of civil rights]. . ."

In response to such criticisms, Rockefeller knew he could always distance himself from the rest of the party due to his background and wealth. Even before the rise of his legendary grandfather, the Rockefellers had distinguished themselves as abolitionists who aided the Underground Railroad, sending slaves to freedom. And after his grandfather accumulated his massive wealth, had it not been for his family's philanthropy, important Negro institutions across the country probably wouldn't even exist. Or if they did, they would do so in facilities vastly inferior to the ones they were in by 1958. Through the years the Rockefellers had done such an exemplary job of covering up for the robber-baron ruthlessness of John senior, to the benefit of people of all colors, that all Nelson had to do was remind audiences that he played no small role in the initiatives, beginning with his role in overseeing the family's gift to New York City during the height of the Great Depression.

By 1958, Rockefeller Center was a fixture in the pantheon of New York City landmarks. It also happened to be headquarters for several blue-chip corporations, including the Radio Corporation of America (RCA), owner of the NBC television station that broadcast a morning show from Rockefeller Center that had taken the nation by storm. The program featured a host who regularly sat with a chimpanzee named J. Fred Muggs, who by 1958 was replaced with another chimp named Mr. Kokomo. Prior to that year, the show was broadcast live while spectators gazed through a large plate glass window into the curbside studio on West 49th Street. Dave Garroway had turned *The Today Show* into an American institution.

Thus, in September 1958, as King prepared to trek to New York City to launch the promotional campaign for *Stride Toward Freedom* in the midst of the governor's race between Harriman and Rockefeller, there was no question that Martin Luther King, Jr., would have to appear on *The Today Show*. An appearance would boost sales of the new book. And there was no question that basking in King's aura would be useful to both gubernatorial candidates. During the days of September 16th to the 20th, the interests of King, Harriman, Rockefeller, and local Negro politicians would all converge. Tuesday, the 16th was the day King made his way to Rockefeller Center to tape his book promotional appearance for *The Today Show*, to be broadcast the following day. That Friday would be the day he would appear with Harriman and Rockefeller, as well as local Negro leaders, on a dais in Harlem in front of the community's historic Hotel Teresa. It would be both Harriman and Rockefeller's third appearance in Harlem that week as they battled each other for the Negro vote. While they prepared to voice the luminous hopeful platitudes always expressed in speeches at such rallies, neither was aware of what would occur the day after the rally. Privately, Harriman—who portrayed himself as more liberal than his Republican opponent— would express himself with far more racial candor, raising many of the same doubts about Negro intelligence that served as the basis for the overt injustices King and the other Montgomery victors were battling in the Deep South. Doubts that would prove so enduring that even after the civil rights movement totally defeated Jim Crow six years later, the questions about Negro intelligence and ability expressed by Harriman regarding what happened to King on the fateful day of September 20, 1958, would remain common among Americans for decades to come. They would endure right up to the present.

putting the right spin
on a huge embarrassment

AS HE PREPARED to make his way to New York City, King and the movement were still basking in their inadvertent success in turning a huge embarrassment into an asset for the movement. During the prior month, autographed, advanced copies of *Stride Toward Freedom* had been sent to several notables, including President Eisenhower, Vice President Nixon, and Chief Justice of the Supreme Court Earl Warren. In the time between handing in the manuscript to Harper and Brothers and receiving finished copies of the book, King was flooded with even more speaking invitations and requests to meet with him in Montgomery from important people around the world. He received a delegation of prominent Indians visiting Montgomery, who echoed what he had written at the end of his book, but in more personal terms:

King would have to be prepared to make physical sacrifices if he was to lead the budding movement as Gandhi had led his. He received correspondence indicating that the editor-in-chief of a major Swedish daily was about to travel to America and that, as part of his study of race relations, Montgomery would be one of his stops and he would like to see King while in the city. Two distinguished Japanese writers were traveling to America, too, intent on making Montgomery one of their stops, eager to meet with King.

Locally, King's right-hand man, Ralph Abernathy, was charged with laying the groundwork for future civil rights protests in Montgomery under the auspices of the MIA. The organization continued to consider suggested new municipal targets of Jim Crow in Montgomery. The most popular idea was to launch a campaign to desegregate the public parks and playgrounds. MIA was preparing the Negro citizens of the city to go to jail for this cause, when, suddenly, it was stymied by the city of Montgomery's response that if it tried to integrate the parks and playgrounds, the facilities would simply be closed.

Like King, Abernathy was pastor of his own church in the city (in fact, the largest Negro church in America). But running MIA and his local church wasn't the only thing the married Abernathy was alleged to be up to. He was also accused of having affairs with his parishioners (years later Abernathy would admit to such infidelities, and accuse King of the same thing, including participating in some of the sexual escapades with him). In that, they were not unlike plenty of prominent married men, such as Harriman's gubernatorial opponent, the married Nelson Rockefeller, and possibly Harriman too, though they were not men of the cloth. And by the end of August (Friday the 29th, to be exact), the husband of one of the women Abernathy was said to be having an affair with appeared at his church brandishing a hatchet and a revolver, warning Abernathy he intended to kill him.

What ensued next was the huge embarrassment that ultimately and inadvertently turned into an asset as King made his way to New York City just a week and a half later. Fleeing his office with blood streaming down his head, Abernathy ran down the street with the husband chasing him in broad daylight still brandishing the gun and hatchet. Soon the police stopped and arrested the man. His wife came down to the station and grew so hysterical that she, too, was arrested under the charge of disorderly conduct. The chastened Abernathy refused to file a complaint. One of the police officers who witnessed the chase filed one instead. Five days later (September 3) along with many of the other Negroes in Montgomery, Martin Luther King, Jr., decided to go to court for the preliminary hearing of the case, in order to show support for his top local assistant. He and his wife, Coretta, accompanied Abernathy and his wife. Upon arriving, they found the courtroom jammed with lines of people waiting to get in. Only Abernathy was allowed inside. King waited outside with his wife and Mrs. Abernathy, hoping Abernathy's lawyer could get him a seat. But the police sergeant who admitted Abernathy commanded King to leave. King peered into the courtroom to see if Abernathy's lawyer was coming to help. At that the sergeant lost his temper, no doubt thinking that just

because King had turned into a world-renowned celebrity for forcing the city to give in to what was, in the sergeant's opinion, a "pre-
posterous" demand, didn't mean King should be accorded special
treatment. In the sergeant's eyes, he was just another nigger. So
he beaconed two officers, who then very roughly seized King as the
Negro spectators gasped in horror, which only encouraged the officers to tighten their grip. The photograph of a young King in a tan
suit and Fedora being manhandled as he stands at the front desk of
the police station house, with his right arm twisted around his back
while his wife looks on in horror, would become one of the most
famous of the entire civil rights movement.

King would be charged with loitering and allowed to post bond.
The following day he was tried, convicted, and ordered to pay a
fourteen-dollar fine. He refused saying he elected to serve time.
But in order to avert further publicity and martyrdom for King,
the city's police commissioner paid his fine instead. Such publicity and martyrdom had come in spades. Roy Wilkins, head of
the NAACP (who privately had mixed feelings about King's rise
along with so many other prominent Negroes of the era), shot off
a telegram to President Eisenhower, admonishing him to make a
statement expressing outrage at King's treatment. Through an
aide, Eisenhower refused, reiterating in a carefully worded letter
that the entire affair was a state concern (evincing no more sympathy for King than his words to Wilkins: "Your interest and concern in this matter are fully understood").

Harriman, by contrast, wouldn't be so shy. He publicly stated,
"The recent arrest and abuse of the Reverend Martin Luther King

was an outrage that dealt our national prestige a damaging blow before the peoples of the world."

His statement was what one could expect from a patrician governor of a relatively liberal state running scared that he might lose the election, eager to mine Negro votes that could prove to be his margin of victory. The rough manhandling of King took the heat off of Abernathy, shifting attention away from the issue of his adulterous liaison, even causing speculation that the incident may have been engineered by enemies of civil rights. As such, the contretemps was chalked up as one more example of the injustices Negroes had to suffer, and the original confrontation that had precipitated it as the embodiment of how low the authorities will stoop in order to hound a civil rights leader. Shrewdly, in line with this interpretation, Abernathy continued to plead his innocence of the affair with the parishioner. And after his Negro lawyer withdrew from the case, the jealous husband was forced to hire the same Caucasian lawyer who had defended the city of Montgomery's segregation policies during the bus boycott, which only added fuel to such an interpretation.

The movement withstood its first major embarrassment. King returned to his hectic schedule, including making preparations for traveling to New York City to promote his book. Little did he know that the shameful scenario of Abernathy and the jilted husband was a mere dress rehearsal for the far more dangerous embarrassment he and the movement would endure in New York City.

taking the kid-glove approach

EXCITEMENT OVER the success of King and the MIA in desegregating Montgomery's buses had caused plenty of people to forget
that not long before, the acronym NAACP stood for the same
degree of daring. Just a year prior to the launch of the boycott,
everyone had been overjoyed at what the NAACP's legal defense
and educational fund had accomplished in winning *Brown v. The
Board of Education.* Despite putting in forty-eight years as the
"radical" alternative to the "go slow" gradualist approach pioneered by Booker T. Washington after the advent of Jim Crow in
the late 1800s; despite laying the legal foundation for challenging
Jim Crow (and offering legal assistance that led to the successful
legal challenge of bus segregation); despite the fact that before
the Montgomery miracle, in plenty of places in the Deep South a

person caught paying dues to the NAACP risked the loss of his livelihood if not his life; at this point the organization looked conservative. For nearly two years now King had been under tremendous pressure to take the movement to its next level. Yet in the midst of the insistent defiance of the school desegregation ruling by Orvall Faubus, and, by comparison, the obedience of the city of Montgomery to a ruling prompted by the bus boycott, he was still treated as the most promising leader. King and his entourage were being counseled by visitors from around the world eager to ally themselves with American Negroes in a struggle that they viewed on an international level; a struggle of non-Caucasian peoples against Western imperialism.

This continuing popularity for King, and the outdated manner in which the NAACP was now painted, was a tough pill to swallow for NAACP Executive Secretary Roy Wilkins. His organization had long preached that activism through the courts—not boycotts, or any other type of civil disobedience—was the only way to topple Jim Crow. Publicly, Wilkins was very careful in dealing with King. Prior to rallying to support King in the embarrassing Abernathy adultery imbroglio, the two had been in frequent contact. Many of the important people eager to visit King in Montgomery first approached the NAACP in New York. And as SCLC got off the ground and the media began reporting stories of competition between the NAACP and SCLC for membership and dues, both strove to refute the stories. They were lying. As soon as the SCLC was formed, Wilkins set to work calling his NAACP field secretaries in the Deep South, to get them to persuade local Negro leaders not to cooperate with King (which may have been one of the reasons SCLC's Crusade for Citizenship voter registration drive was such a disappointment). He was especially in touch with his Mississippi Field Secretary Medgar Evers, who busily obeyed his directive. And that King was so young compared to Wilkins (who was fifty-one) didn't help matters any. Neither did the fact that after so many years of working hard to expunge the NAACP of any hint of association with Communists (even NAACP Legal Defense and Educational Fund Director Thurgood Marshall served as an informant for the FBI), King was introducing people into the movement who made Wilkins nervous (long after the movement was over it would be revealed that King's most important non Afro-American adviser, Stanley Levison, was indeed a Communist at the time he aided King).

Nevertheless, it would look quite bad if, while King was in New York City, someone from the NAACP didn't demonstrate some modicum of public cordiality. Wilkins decided not to join the list of notables who would sit on the dais of the rally to be held in front of the Hotel Teresa in Harlem on Friday, September 19. Besides Harriman and Rockefeller, joining King would be baseball great Jackie Robinson; A. Phillip Randolph; Duke Ellington, whose band would provide music for the rally; Manhattan Borough President Hulan Jack; and Reverend Gardner Taylor, pastor of Concord Baptist Church in Brooklyn. Conspicuously absent would be Harlem Congressman Adam Clayton Powell, Jr. And none of the heavyweights from the NAACP would be there. Other officers in the organization realized it would look very bad if someone didn't make a public gesture of some kind. One such person was Arthur Spingarn, the organization's eighty-year-old Jewish president.

Spingarn and his brother, Joel, were so important to the early days of the NAACP and the early fight for racial justice that they deserved to be considered as integral to laying the groundwork as A. Phillip Randolph, W.E.B. Du Bois, Walter White, James Weldon Johnson, Ida B. Wells, and all the other men and women who carried the torch prior to the rise of King. The NAACP's highest award, the Spingarn Medal—which would become the equivalent of the Nobel Peace Prize in the Negro world—would be named for Joel. Both brothers joined not long after the organization was formed in 1910, primarily by a coalition of Caucasians alarmed at the racial atrocities taking place in the early twentieth century. (Though this coalition included Du Bois, he came along shortly after the first meetings were held and, of course, played a defining role upon joining.) Among the founders was Oswald Garrison Villard, grandson of the famed pre–Civil War abolitionist William Lloyd Garrison (who was instrumental in launching the career of Frederick Douglass). Villard was publisher of *The Nation* magazine and the *New York Evening Post*. In the early days of the NAACP, he provided free rent to the organization in the same Fifth Avenue building that housed *The Nation*. While suffering through the boredom of working for a private law firm on, of all issues (in light of the source of wealth for Averell Harriman's family), the reorganization of railroads, Arthur was approached by Villard to take a civil rights case. Upon doing so, he caught the civil rights bug and ended up chairing the NAACP's legal committee (precursor to its Legal Defense and Educational Fund) shortly after its formation, serving in that capacity for twenty-seven years, winning eleven cases before the U.S. Supreme Court. Then in 1940, Arthur became president of the organization.

At the beginning of their involvement, the Spingarns often encountered people who were amazed at their commitment. During debates on the subject of Negro intelligence, Caucasian acquaintances would say to the younger Spingarn, "You say the Negro has the same capabilities as the white. What books has he written?" In response to this, Arthur started collecting books by Negro authors. (By 1966 his collection of 3,000 would be donated to UCLA.) Through most of the first half of the 20th century, the Greenwich Village home he shared with his wife (they'd have no children) was a stopover for notable New York intellectuals, writers, and artists such as Eugene O'Neill and John Sloan. After the death of Booker T. Washington in 1915, Arthur and his brother (with heavy influence from Du Bois) organized a famous civil rights conclave for notable Negro activists and intellectuals on the grounds of Joel's Amenia, New York, residence. To be known as the Amenia Conference, virtually everyone of consequence on the race issue in those days was present, representing the full spectrum of opinions on the subject. Designed to bring the Bookerite faction of the movement together with those who believed in agitating for immediate rights, in the end the conference didn't bring many of the

Bookerites into the fold. Except for one key man. Not long after it ended, poet, composer, lawyer, author, and diplomat James Weldon Johnson would join the NAACP, assuming the newly created office of national field secretary, which eventually became the office of executive secretary, a position held next by an insurance salesman from Atlanta named Walter White; then after White, a journalist from Kansas City by the name of Roy Wilkins. The same man who now nervously contemplated the phenomenon of Martin Luther King, Jr.

Under the constitution of the NAACP, the president had very little power. Most authority resided with the executive secretary. Ever since the days of Johnson it had been up to the executive secretary to serve as the principal face of the organization, dealing with the myriad matters his role required him to address: fund-raising, speaking engagements, traveling to the latest racial hotspots, keeping local chapters in line with national policy, and now, with the rise of King and his followers and allies, serving as informal envoy between such "hotheads" and high government officials who might listen to the head of the NAACP before they would leaders of other Negro organizations.

As far as King's recent arrest was concerned, both Wilkins and Spingarn no doubt knew that a telegram to President Eisenhower hoping he would express outrage was merely a cosmetic gesture, intended more to cover their own tracks when someone asked what they had done than anything else. For three decades, Spingarn had consulted with every U.S. president on the issue of civil rights, and knew that Eisenhower was only doing the bare minimum required by the recent decisions of the Supreme Court. He claimed that once, during an audience with the president, in which he asked for a civil rights favor, Eisenhower replied, "I haven't got the time to do it. I'm too tired. Now today I had to sign fifteen important matters and only had five minutes to make a decision on the fifteenth. I ought to have had two weeks on each." To Spingarn, this reply indicated that Eisenhower didn't really know what he was doing as he performed his duties.

As for the phenomenon of King, Spingarn took the long view. He realized that the NAACP's expenses had increased tremendously as a result of aiding the budding activism in the Deep South. And he also worried about the activists King was bringing into the movement, fearful that Communists were slipping through. They had long been a problem at certain NAACP local chapter meetings, making outlandish motions while genuine members were present. Then they'd wait until the genuine members left, make the motions again, and get them passed, after which national headquarters would have to send someone down to straighten everything out.

But this wasn't the issue at the moment for eighty-year-old Spingarn. The issue now was how to make it clear to the public and press that there was no friction between the NAACP and King since Wilkins wasn't going to be on the dais at Friday's Harlem rally. The solution lay in the fact that the following day King was scheduled to sign books right around the corner from where the rally was held: Blumstein's Department Store on 125th Street. Spingarn, the dean of the NAACP, decided to be there for a public photo opportunity with King. For King to have his picture taken next to Spingarn would be like a young Frederick Douglass taking a photograph next to his elder and mentor, William Lloyd Garrison. Little did Spingarn realize that one of the photos taken of him next to King would, indeed, go down in history. But not for the reasons he had hoped.

FIVE

why isn't king signing books at my bookstore?

IN THE EYES of one of Harlem's legends, it seemed pretty strange and insulting for King to agree to sign books during his visit in a Harlem department store that didn't even sell books. On top of that, a department store that wasn't even Negro-owned. And this in a community that was considered the capital of Negro America. When people around the world thought of Negro accomplishment in literature and entertainment, they thought of Harlem. They thought of the names of those who had illuminated it as the shining beacon of what they viewed as best about the Negro—poet Countee Cullen; poet and author Langston Hughes; the author, composer, and lawyer that the Spingarn's Amenia Conference bought into the NAACP fold, James Weldon Johnson; singer and actor Paul Robeson; author Arna Bontemps; scholar and librarian

Arthur Schomburg; the composer and bandleader who was to play at the rally in front of the Hotel Teresa, Duke Ellington; jazz saxophonist Charlie Parker; jazz vocalist Sarah Vaughan. . . . And those *really in the know* when considering Harlem legends also thought of bookstore owner Lewis Michaeux.

In the 1920s while Arthur Spingarn was still producing, for doubters among his Caucasian contemporaries, books by Negro authors proving Negro intelligence, Lewis Michaeaux was hunting basements in the homes of Harlem friends in search of the same type of books to display on his pushcart and sell to other Negroes. It seemed that pioneering was in his family's blood. His younger brother, Elder Solomon "Lightfoot" Micheaux, would become known as the "Happy Am I" preacher who allegedly became wealthy from the enthusiastic response to his Radio Church of God, and a real estate empire that included churches worth millions of dollars. Michaeux also happened to be the cousin of a Micheaux who had pioneered in the world of film. Oscar Micheaux's name would go down in history for his early films about Negro cowboys; domestic bliss and tragedy amongst Negroes; historical films about Negro accomplishment, and so on; before finally succumbing to the monopolistic ways of Hollywood. Had this other Micheaux not been cruelly crushed, had he found the financial and behind-the-scenes support obtained by men with last names like Cohn, Goldwyn, Mayer, and so on, whose studios became Hollywood legends, there is no telling how far Negro achievement in a variety of arenas might have spread. The same could have been said during the height of the Harlem Renaissance for gangsters squeezed out of the clandestine activities they pioneered. In the numbers racket, for example, Bumpy Johnson was replaced by the likes of Mafiosi such as Lucky Luciano, who, in turn, helped finance posh entertainment outlets like the Cotton Club, which featured the music of Duke Ellington and the hedonistic shimmying of the cafe-au-lait Cotton Club dancers for the pleasure of prosperous Caucasians only, eagerly "slumming" up in Harlem. Johnson, too, might have plowed clandestine wealth into the entertainment industry. There were all kinds of "what ifs" to consider when one really stopped to think about things. And Lewis Michaeux, to the consternation of plenty of Negroes considered more pragmatic, was always stopping to think about things and doing something in protest after thinking as long and hard as he thought necessary.

Born near Newport News, Virginia, in 1884, Micheaux migrated to New York City in his early twenties. After saving enough money from selling books from his Harlem pushcart, in 1930 he opened a bookstore on Seventh Avenue, near the corner of 125th Street, catty-corner from where King was to speak twenty-eight years later at the September 19th rally; the spot became known as Harlem Square due to the constant political activity that took place there. Through the years activists of all kinds harangued passersby with their political agendas (beginning in the 1940s, when 125th Street stores were integrated and the center of Negro Harlem moved from 135th Street and Lenox Avenue to 125th Street and Seventh Avenue, the political street activists moving with the tide). Michaeux called his bookstore the National

Memorial African Bookstore and, in the beginning, slept in the back and washed windows for people when proceeds from selling his books couldn't make ends meet. Eventually, proceeds did make ends meet and he maintained what for most of the next twenty-eight years was the only bookstore in Harlem. During Christmas season, the bookstore would sell as many as five hundred Bibles to the community. It would also earn a reputation as the most comprehensive bookshop on Negroes in the world. Over time it would earn the informal name of "The House of Common Sense and Proper Propaganda"—the words displayed on a sign Michaeux placed in the front window. The National Memorial African Bookstore became a meeting place for students, scholars, African diplomats, and politicians. All kinds of books about Negroes were stacked up to its high ceiling. And there were portraits of famed Negro men and women, too. Harlem Square street activists often stopped in to check historical claims about the Negro before mounting their ladders and haranguing the crowds of pedestrians. Langston Hughes and Countee Cullen often stopped by to discuss with the small, wiry bespectacled Michaeux the hardships of being a Negro writer; others who stopped by included Joe Louis, Sugar Ray Robinson; Louis Armstrong; W.E.B. Du Bois (when he was still living in America before moving to Ghana); and the irascible Harlem congressman and pastor of historic Abyssinian Baptist Church, Adam Clayton Powell, Jr.

Yet perhaps it was Micheaux's reputation for militancy that caused King to avoid signing books at his store. This was the man who featured on his bookshelves not only titles with verifiable facts about the Negro but also those making dubious romantic claims about black African history that any person who thought hard about the Negro predicament would find understandable. You shove an entire people off into a corner with nothing more to glue them together as a group than just one detectable drop of ancestry from sub-Saharan Africa—ancestry from a multitude of West African ethnicities, no matter how much ancestry they harbor from elsewhere (the equivalent of defining as Caucasian anyone with one drop of ancestry from Western Europe, meaning that under such a definition the vast majority of American Negroes would then become Caucasian)—it only made sense that the said people would feel compelled to find any means they could to be proud of what glued them together. Michaeux's bookstore was the epicenter of not only respected Negro scholars researching their work but also those who still upheld the ideals of Marcus Garvey (Michaeux himself was still a Garveyite), and those who followed the teachings of Elijah Muhammad, founder of the Nation of Islam. These facts indicate the complexities of Lewis Michaeux.

One year he featured in the window of his store a large sign about a new book entitled *The Goddamn White Man*. He received a lot of complaints about the sign. Caucasians began writing him, the local police began bugging him. A Caucasian officer said, "Now, look, you have an institute of learning here, and this is a bad thing for young folks to be seeing—you cursing the white man."

"Well, I'm going to sell the book as long as the publisher is publishing it," replied Michaeux. "You see the publisher and stop them, then I won't sell the book."

Due to his refusal to stop advertising the book in the window, the police department sent him a summons to show cause for not removing the sign. Michaeux showed up in court with a Webster's Dictionary picking out various words to define the meaning of freedom of speech, successfully demonstrating why he had a right to feature the sign and sell the book.

It was easy to understand why association with such a controversial man would be a potential problem for an emerging leader like King, who preached nonviolence and echoed Jesus's teaching to love your enemy, to turn the other cheek. The powers-that-be were already watching King closely for potential Communist infiltration among his ranks. Did it make sense to help launch his book at a Harlem bookstore that might add fuel to their suspicions?

Micheaux didn't see things this way. He felt that his bookstore was a natural setting for a book signing by King. So he put in a call to Montgomery inquiring if King wanted to have one. But to his surprise no one called him back. He put in calls to the appropriate people in New York City. Again, there was no response.

That's strange, thought Michaeux. Surely this young product of Morehouse College, of the educated Negro middle class, was aware of who he was. And if he wasn't, certainly there were enough people around him who could have enlightened him. As time passed and each day he heard nothing from King, King's publisher, or any of King's emissaries, Lewis Micheaux grew increasingly perplexed, increasingly miffed, increasingly angry. The political rally featuring King, Rockefeller, Harriman, and a host of other notables was going to take place catty-corner from his bookstore, but there would be no signing? And other events were planned for King elsewhere in Harlem. The day before the rally, he was scheduled to sign books at a new establishment in the community called the Empire State Bookstore, operated by the Empire State Baptist Missionary Convention. He would also appear at a Harlem church. Then the day after the rally he would sign copies at Blumstein's, a Jewish-owned department store around the corner that didn't even sell books. Upon pondering this obvious snub, Michaeux's anger became a boiling cauldron.

Though King had experienced a meteoric rise in popularity among Negroes across the country, he was coming into the community that had set the pace for theorizing on how the collective future of Negroes should proceed, and snubbing the very epicenter for such activity, which was owned by a seventy-four-year-old man who had been fighting for racial justice in his own way a lot longer than King had been. Thus Micheaux felt no qualms about embarrassing King as he visited the community. He felt no qualms about challenging King on why his bookstore was being overlooked. As it became clear that he wouldn't be hearing from King or anyone connected with him, that's precisely what Lewis Micheaux prepared to do.

not quite in touch with reality

AS LEADERS OF the NAACP knew only too well, the other issue turning the minds of the American people upside down in those days was
Communism. Communists enjoyed popularity in the country during
the Great Depression. Americans of all colors who had been rendered
destitute searched for the ultimate safety net. Young idealists in academia, the labor movement, and the arts turned to Karl Marx as the
savior. After World War II came, postwar prosperity followed for the
victorious United States. At the same time, citizens witnessed the brutal manner in which Communist Russia took over Eastern Europe.
The result was a national fear of Communism. Senator Joe McCarthy
and the House Un-American Activities Committee (HUAC) domi-
nated the news. From 1951 to 1954, HUAC destroyed the careers of
numerous former young idealists now repentant and eager to enjoy

postwar prosperity. By 1958, McCarthy's witch-hunt was dead, yet America was still obsessed with the Red Scare. And since both Socialists and Communists preached institutionalized equality, it was only natural for critics of the civil rights movement to equate civil rights with Socialism and Communism. And just as natural for Socialists and Communists to gravitate toward the civil rights movement.

As Wilkins and Spingarn knew only too well, civil rights leaders were always being called Communist agents. Hence, Thurgood Marshall's willingness to spy for the FBI, assuring J. Edgar Hoover of the NAACP's bona fides. Distinguished Negroes eager to prove they were good Americans were always being forced to straddle the need to assure the powers-that-be that they were good capitalists with their passion for racial equality. There had long been the need to reconcile the theory that private businesses had a right to serve whoever they pleased, with the conviction that no one should be excluded from such service due to race or gender. King's agenda during the Montgomery bus boycott and the theory under which *Brown v. The Board of Education* had been won, of course, fell outside of this purview since they both dealt not with private enterprise but with public services. Yet on the horizon for the movement was the issue of Negro treatment by private businesses as well (by 1960 the lunch counter sit-ins at five-and-dime department stores would be launched by Negro college students in North Carolina). As the movement continued to gain momentum, the most respected Negro leaders distanced themselves from known Communists. People like King adviser Stanley Levison did their best to conceal their Communist backgrounds from the general public.

Simultaneously, paranoids came out of the woodwork to hound leaders of the movement. One was a tall, large-boned, dark-skinned forty-two-year-old Negro woman with a restless nature named Izola Curry. Born near the tiny hamlet of Adrian, Georgia, to a mother and father who were sharecroppers, the grown-up Curry, now residing in New York City, had a taste for baubly earrings and expensive eyeglasses. For that day and age, she was a fashion plate. Izola had been one of five children (three boys and two girls), and attended elementary school in nearby Savannah until the third grade. In 1937 she married. But six months later she left her husband, fled to New York City, and kept the last name Curry. She began dating a man named Leroy Weekes, who eventually asked her to marry him. She refused. Apparently Weekes had become involved to some extent in the NAACP.

Like plenty of others in those days, Curry believed the NAACP was controlled by Communists. But in her increasingly deranged state of mind, unlike paranoids such as J. Edgar Hoover, she sought no evidence of such a connection. She simply assumed as much. She assumed that Communists were running things in every civil rights organization.

By 1956 paranoia had gotten the best of her. She began writing the FBI claiming that Communist agents were out to get her. She fled numerous cities, living for a time in Cleveland; St. Louis; Charleston, West Virginia; back again in Savannah; then West Palm Beach, Florida; Lexington, Kentucky; Columbia, South Carolina; Miami; Daytona Beach, and back again to New York City. By September 1958, she was renting a room in a brownstone at 121 West 122nd Street in Harlem, which she paid for by working at various places when she could as a temp maid. And when not working, she continued to express extreme bitterness about two things: Communism and the Negro Church. She especially detested Negro preachers. Curry felt that they were flimflam artists who pimped the community. She believed that boycotts and protests led by Negro ministers were a sham and that rather than follow them into protests, Negroes should appeal directly to Congress to change the racial laws. Thus in Curry's mind, Martin Luther King, Jr., was a young minister pimping the community for the benefit of Communists.

To her neighbors she was a very antisocial woman. Curry spoke with a distinct Southern accent, but her words were often unintelligible and ungrammatical. When Curry could be understood, she was often heard expressing not only hatred for Negro preachers and Communists but for "whites," too. Those around her simply wrote her off as one of the eccentric types. It was hardly unusual to run into her kind in a city the size of New York. She just happened to be Harlem's contribution.

Perusing the newspapers, Curry found out about the upcoming trip King was to make to the city and his scheduled appearance at a political rally very near where she lived. She made note of it and decided to attend so that she could give King a piece of her mind. She decided to tail him as much as she could as he toured the community. Izola Curry decided to settle once and for all what she viewed as the silly business of Communist-influenced protests being led by a licentious Negro preacher intent on ruining the country.

stride toward critical acclaim

THE NEW YORKERS King encountered on September 15, 1958, upon arriving in the city were eager to embrace the nascent civil rights movement. As he traveled the city, King would be greeted by pre-dominantly Negro crowds ready to denounce his recent arrest in Montgomery, ready to support the integration of public schools in Little Rock, Arkansas, ready to grant points to gubernatorial opponents Averell Harriman and Nelson Rockefeller for taking positions in support of the movement as they squared off against each other. Caucasian New Yorkers, on the other hand, were less enthusiastic, yet not hostile. For the most part they paid lip service to the notion that Negroes were true equals. Outside of the Deep South, where de facto rather than de jure segregation was the rule, even among liberal Caucasians, slow, primarily symbolic progress was as far as they were willing to take things. Most residents, for example, were just getting used to the type of progress made by New York–based Mohawk Airlines in hiring the first Negro flight attendant in the entire airline industry to serve passengers on its DC-3 flights from New York City to Buffalo. This didn't mean that major airlines intended to make a concerted effort to hire many more Negro flight attendants (there was no such thing as affirmative action back then). It merely meant that a beachhead of slow progress had been established, and for now that was enough.

By contrast, in much of the America of 1958 beyond the boundaries of New York City and the rest of the East Coast, espousing a belief in Negro equality automatically aroused suspicion that you were a member of the same Communist party that J. Edgar Hoover and Izola Curry worried about night and day. Negroes were still *them;* something akin to aliens, due to their dark skin (darkness, it was stated throughout Judeo-Christian theology, was the mark of evil, of doom), kinky hair, broad noses, thick lips. Thus even when the typical Caucasian saw a person whose features were similar to his but who shared just one physical characteristic with a Negro, that person was deemed a Negro. And, the thinking went, if anyone needed any further evidence to back up the assertion of Negro inferiority, they need only witness the backwardness of Negroes on the continent they originated from: Africa. Where was Negro civilization? Who was the Tolstoy of the Zulus? The Albert Einstein? The Leonardo Da Vinci? The Louis Pasteur?

When Martin Luther King, Jr., landed in the media capital of America to promote his new book, the challenge was to convince most of the nation that the country hadn't been built solely for Caucasian individuals. The challenge was to convince most Caucasians that supporting Negro rights wasn't tantamount to sup- porting the Kremlin. By September 1958, the idea that Gotham was the country's media capital, open to the expression of new ideas, originated largely from the fact that the city had always been a polyglot of immigrants from around the world, forced to deal with each other because the designated *them* freshly off the latest passenger ship docked at Ellis Island might live only a block away stacked in a tenement around the corner from your own tenement. The city's massive size necessitated the largest, most ambitious public works projects in the country—a comprehensive city hos- pital system, the most extensive and sophisticated public school system (including colleges and universities), gargantuan public housing complexes, bridges, mass transit systems. In New York City, the concept of the collective good had long existed in tandem with the rights of the individual, and it remained that way even during the post–World War II economic boom. In the rest of the nation, however, a sense of the collective good (as it applied to Caucasians) only enjoyed popularity during economic hard times (the inequality and horrendous working conditions of the Industrial Revolution, the Great Depression, and so on), only to recede once prosperity returned. In many ways, you might say, the typical New Yorker viewed group rights as superseding individual rights, even though the group he usually fought for was his own. And what added to the prevailing atmosphere in the city during the post–World War II years was the primacy attached to a mission of justice for the oppressed emanating from the 1.5 million Jews living in the city, by far the largest Jewish community in the nation.

For these reasons New York City, including the outer boroughs, always seemed like foreign territory to the rest of America, physically and mentally set off, lying on three islands off the coast of the continent (except for the Bronx) divided into something strange called "boroughs." And there was the typical New Yorker arrogance and brashness. Manhattan's massive collection of skyscrapers were a wonder to behold, from which corporate managers wielded the straws that stirred the economic fluid of the country. Yet they didn't represent the spirit of the nation. Rather, in the interest of profits, they *played to the nation's spirit.* With condescension, yes. "Will it play in Peoria?"; "How will Dorothy in Kansas receive it?" However, every once in a while, among the media occupying these office towers, attempts were made to enlighten the rest of America. In an effort to explain what the Montgomery revolt was all about, the publicity department of Harper and Brothers set about promoting King's book.

On September 17, 1958, the official day of publication, the *New York Herald Tribune's* Maurice Dolbier, who reviewed books in the same section where the editorials and columns of that august newspaper were featured (among them, the opinions of the nation's most eminent journalist, Walter Lippmann), spoke glowingly of it. In the center of what he had to say was a portrait of twenty-nine-year-old King in suit and tie, looking pleasant and distinguished. But elsewhere in that prestigious organ of journalism in the nation's most liberal city, support for the idea King's

Montgomery victory represented was mixed. To the far left of Dolbier's review, columnist Roscoe Drummond asked, "Will Integration Mean End of the South's Public Schools?", a piece apropos of the ongoing controversy in Little Rock.

It was *understandable that a community would want to avoid integration*, wrote Drummond. But only if it could do so without penalty. The way Drummond saw it, the Supreme Court had made its decision, and the need for public schools superseded any aversion for Negroes because public schools were a dire necessity if the United States was to produce "more scientists, more engineers, more scholars to meet the scientific and industrial challenge of Communist imperialism." Despite Drummond's opinion, the order of the day across the country was still thick with belief that individual liberty for Caucasians ought to win out over collective liberty for Negroes. In the column to the immediate left of Dolbier's review, David Lawrence, based in Washington, noted that many people were writing in to him trying to learn more about "the dubious origins of the Fourteenth Amendment [to the Constitution]—supposed basis of the desegregation decisions—to which reference was recently made in these dispatches." That amendment, ratified in 1868, guaranteed the newly freed slaves equal protection under the law. And Lawrence insisted that in 1868 the state legislatures that ratified it were of doubtful legitimacy because so many of them were made up of Negroes in Southern states who had been elected to serve in the state capitols through the federal government's questionable Reconstruction policies. Ninety years after the fact, Lawrence was implying that

the South, at the time, had been under the spell of Negro bar-
barism and chaos.

Martin Luther King had been in town for two days when this
particular issue of the *Herald Tribune* hit the newsstands. The previous day he had taped his appearance with Dave Garroway on *The
Today Show*. As the *Herald Tribune* review of the book appeared, his
interview with Garroway was aired. The two men were seen in a
pleasant, informative, hopeful conversation in which King reiterated his concept of nonviolence. After the taping, King made his
way back to the Hotel Statler where he was staying.

The next day he made his way to Harlem to sign copies of his
new book at the Empire State Bookstore. After the signing he
again mingled with admirers. Then that evening he made his way
to a rally held at Williams Institutional CME Church, also in
Harlem. Originally planned to raise money for the Crusade for
Citizenship—the voter registration drive King was organizing
through SCLC—it turned instead into a rally to support King himself due to the embarrassment the movement had suffered
because of the Abernathy fiasco.

King drank in the sympathy of the parishioners, who displayed
one more example of the rousing emotionalism characteristic of
Negro worship services. A succession of speakers preceded King,
including not just the pastor of Williams Institutional but also
Dr. Thomas Kilgore, pastor of the Friendship Baptist Church,
sponsors of the evening. King electrified the overflow crowd of
eight hundred people. The collection plate was passed, and $1,100
was raised for SCLC. Then King socialized some more with admir-

ers, answering their questions. Afterward he retired to the Hotel Statler and rested for the following day's political rally on the corner of 125th Street and Seventh Avenue in front of Harlem's historic Hotel Teresa.

The next day, as the crowd gathered for the rally, besides containing hostile persons such as Lewis Micheaux and Izola Curry, there were others in the audience who could hardly be expected to welcome King's message of nonviolence. Since the beginning of the twentieth century when the Harlem real estate bust began, causing speculators to begin renting apartments and rooms to Negroes, Negroes from throughout the diaspora—the West Indies, the Deep South, and Africa—had been attracted to the community, bringing with them a variety of political viewpoints they felt far freer to express than Negroes were able to elsewhere in the country. As stated earlier, the street-corner orators venting these opinions started out on the corner of 135th Street and Lenox Avenue (from approximately 1917 to the early 1940s). Then, once the Caucasian-owned stores on 125th Street were integrated, compliments of the civil rights protests of the Reverend Adam Clayton Powell, Jr., the soapbox orators migrated down. Most of them tended to do as all street-corner orators do—espouse views at odds with those of the prevailing establishment in their communities. In 1918, the prevailing establishment among Negro leaders in the Northeast had converted to the point of view of the NAACP. At that time the organization had decided to subordinate its call for immediate civil rights, and call instead on Negroes to faithfully serve their country on the battlefields of World War I, under the theory that once Negroes proved their patriotism, the civil rights struggle would then be far easier. One of the soapbox orators who spoke out in complete opposition to that point of view was A. Phillip Randolph. By Friday, September 19, 1958, A. Phillip Randolph was now considered the dean among established Negro leaders, and as such would mount the stage with King at the scheduled political rally in front of the Hotel Teresa.

While Randolph was busy organizing his labor union in the 1920s, the Marcus Garveyites began dazzling the masses on the same street corner Randolph had enthralled them on. Garvey's followers organized themselves into the Universal Negro Improvement Association (UNIA), promoting their "back to Africa movement" with fantasies of Negro glory complete with military pageantry. Under a different agenda (minus the military pageantry and espousal of absolute separatism, yet every bit as insistent on Negro freedom), Harlem Congressman Adam Clayton Powell, Jr., delivered the street-corner orations that would gain him the renown that would return him time and time again first to the New York City Council and then to the U.S. Congress, representing Harlem. And very shortly it would be in this manner that Malcolm X, King's most serious rival for the hearts and minds of young Afro-Americans, espoused the black Muslim point of view.

Once the epicenter of the exhortations moved to Seventh Avenue and 125th Street, ideologues constantly jostled for attention. And unlike in the Deep South, none of the speakers had any qualms about calling for the complete destruction of Caucasian America. But the corner was also a place from which established

Harlem leaders (elected officials) often spoke along with invited guests such as other New York politicians and national political leaders. During such rallies traffic was closed off and crowds were allowed to fill the intersection and the space directly in front of the Hotel Teresa, the stately twelve-story white structure dominating the Harlem horizon. Yet whoever spoke had to be ready for anything. Harlem was the toughest spot in America (perhaps the entire world) for any aspiring Negro leader or ally of Negroes, just as right around the corner from the Hotel Teresa, the Apollo Theater was the toughest nut for any Negro to crack in the entertainment industry. If you could win a crowd over in Harlem, you could win one over anywhere.

Friday evening of September 19th arrived, and King prepared to win over an even bigger slice of Harlem to his activist point of view. Governor Harriman and his phalanx of aides arrived first and mounted the stage. Later came Rockefeller and his entourage. Both made their way through the throng, hopeful that they would convince enough voters of the rightness of their respective messages; hopeful that their third visit to Harlem in a week would pay off as listeners tried to decide which one of them had been the better friend of Negroes.

Shortly after they took their places on stage, King and his aides made their entrance. They were flanked by Manhattan Borough President Hulan Jack, baseball great Jackie Robinson, A. Phillip Randolph, and Reverend Gardner Taylor. Duke Ellington stood at the base of the dais and prepared to conduct his band. Soon the music began, and afterward the introductions were made.

Robinson spoke first. Referring to the upcoming election, the dashingly handsome dark-skinned slugger intoned, "We are the balance of power." Gesturing behind himself toward Harriman and Rockefeller, to the thunderous applause of the audience he continued, "We can put Governor Harriman back in office or we can put Mr. Rockefeller in. I'm sure these two gentlemen realize the tremendous potential of you and me." Next came the words of Randolph, who criticized the civil rights record of President Eisenhower, accusing him of going slow on integration and emphasizing the cautious manner in which he had handled the school desegregation quagmire in Little Rock. In a fiery follow-up to Randolph's words, Gardner Taylor leveled the same criticism. Then it was time for the next speaker.

Though Governor Harriman had arrived before him, Rockefeller spoke before Harriman. Cognizant of the fact that he was compelled to show at least some degree of party loyalty, he decided that he had no alternative but to defend Eisenhower, who only a week earlier, after the Supreme Court issued its ruling ordering the integration of Little Rock schools, released a statement that merely called upon the citizens of the city to obey the decision. Plenty of people took this to mean that Eisenhower was lukewarm on the issue of integration (which, indeed, he was).

"This business about [Eisenhower] going slow on integration," Rockefeller asserted in the raconteurish manner that would become his trademark over the years. "I know the man! I worked with him. . . . Who sent the troops to Little Rock? That takes courage in this country."

Then he tried to steer attention away from the national Republican party and back to his own more liberal attitude. "We cannot rewrite the laws in Arkansas," he intoned. "But we can embark on a bold program to solve the problems in our own state. We have a proud record of combating prejudice based on race, creed, and color."

As Rockefeller continued, there was one heckler in particular making herself a nuisance. Izola Curry appeared behind the stage in a nice dress and her trademark expensive eyewear. While listening to Rockefeller, she voiced her hatred of Caucasians. William Rowe, an assistant to Borough President Hulan Jack who served as King's escort while in the city, did his best to calm her down. And Frederick Weaver, a platform guest, motioned for police officers to make her stop. But the police were reluctant to get tough with her, fearing that to do so might start an incident among the throng of five thousand Harlemites that could escalate into a larger racial disturbance. Rockefeller finished his speech, declaring to great applause, "Let's take civil rights out of the talk stage and put it in the active stage!"

Now it was Harriman's turn. Invoking the names of Harry Truman and Franklin Roosevelt—the two Democratic presidents whose policies were responsible for catalyzing a sea change in the attitude of Afro-Americans toward the Democratic party after so many years of loyalty to the Republicans as the party of Abraham Lincoln—he continued the references to the Little Rock crisis begun by the others. He criticized Eisenhower for waiting so long a year earlier, when the crisis began, before sending in the

National Guard to ensure the safety of the six young Negro students integrating Little Rock Central High School. These students had to withstand the jeers and violence of Caucasian spectators while a national television audience watched in horror. "For three weeks [Eisenhower] waited. Well, I ask you, my friends, how long would it have taken Harry Truman?"

"One day!" responded the crowd. Then he criticized the president for refraining from stating that the Supreme Court school desegregation decision should be obeyed not only because it was now the law but because it was also morally right, and that his failure to do this created a vacuum into which bigots and demagogues felt free to move.

As he said this, Izola Curry started up again calling Caucasians racists. Once more Rowe tried to calm her down.

Soon it was King's turn. And Lewis Michaeux, with twelve supporters in tow, let King know how he felt about being snubbed. At the Empire State Bookstore the day before, it was estimated that King autographed at the rate of three books per minute and signed a total of five hundred copies. "I've been here for twenty-two years as the leading Negro bookstore in Harlem," complained Michaeux to a reporter. "And yet King and his publishers didn't even come to see me."

King ignored Michaeux and his supporters and delivered his prepared remarks. He voiced support for integrating the Little Rock schools, calling upon the federal government to step in and take over if necessary. "Many of you had hoped I would come here to bring you a message of hate against the white man because of what has happened," he continued, obviously referring to what happened to him during the Abernathy fiasco. "I come with no such message. Black supremacy is just as bad as white supremacy." This utterance was met with mingled applause. "I come with a message of love rather than hate," he continued. What he said next would become a standard refrain throughout his days as the principal disciple of nonviolence in the movement: "Don't let any man make you stoop so low that you have hate. Have love in your hearts for those who would do you wrong." Surprisingly, in light of the fact that this was Harlem, cheers for these words rose to a crescendo, drowning out the jeers of Izola Curry, who had started up her heckling once more, protesting that no Negro should ever try to cooperate with a Caucasian.

Miraculously, the rally ended without incident. But Hulan Jack was worried. He felt that in light of the heckling of Curry as well as Michaeux and his supporters, it was probably best for King to have a bodyguard for the remainder of his visit. He told King and Rowe this as the three of them stepped off the dais. "Oh God, don't get a bodyguard!" King is alleged to have responded. Then, turning to Rowe, he said, "And don't you try to act like one either."

In light of what happened the following day, the three men would regret this decision.

crisis

SATURDAY, SEPTEMBER 20th was a beautiful sunny day. William Rowe made his way back to the Hotel Statler in midtown to pick up King and escort him to Blumstein's. As he waited for King to arrive, Mr. I. B. Blumstein was a little nervous. The previous evening Micheaux's supporters had picketed the store urging passersby to "Buy Black." What if they reappeared? wondered Blumstein, who had a couple of police present just in case. Luckily no one came.

As they awaited King's arrival, store employees set up a desk behind the shoe department. A photographer from Harper and Brothers also waited to take photos of King with various VIPs and others waiting for him to sign copies of his book. Short, elderly, bespectacled Arthur Spingarn waited too, along with about fifty other people, including an honor guard of female students from a local junior high school. Finally King, Rowe, and the rest of their entourage made their way inside. The decision was made that the first order of business was to take a photo of King and Spingarn together. As the photos were taken with King sitting at the desk, Spingarn standing above him, King smiling and turning to shake Spingarn's hand, the fifty other people present patiently formed a line and waited their turns to have copies of their books signed. It was about 3:30 P.M. Suddenly Izola Curry waded through the throng, wearing her trademark earrings, sequined spectacles, and a nice dress covered by a blue raincoat. Under her coat she brandished a slender Japanese penknife with a gently curving blade six to eight inches long and a handle made of inlaid ivory. She also had a loaded Italian-made .32-caliber automatic pistol in her purse.

"Is this Martin Luther King?" she asked as she walked straight up to King, hands concealed in her raincoat. "Yes it is," replied King, certain this was just one more of the many fans he had been greeting for four days. Suddenly Curry brought her hand out of her raincoat in an arc. Instinctively, King yanked his left arm up to block the letter opener, cutting his left hand as Curry plunged the blade into his chest. Quickly a bystander knocked Curry's hand away from the blade before she could pull it out and stab King again. "I've been after him for six years!" shouted Curry. "I'm glad I done it!" Curry started to run. A group of women who had been flanking King began chasing her, brandishing umbrellas and shouting, "Catch her! Don't let her go!" Before they could reach her, the store's floor manager blocked their path. Walter Pettiford, an advertising executive for the *New York Amsterdam News*, the city's principal Negro-owned newspaper, grabbed Curry's left arm and swung her around so that he could grab her other arm. Then he proceeded to lead her toward the front of the store hoping to locate a store detective. As he held her, Curry kept repeating, "Dr. King has ruined my life! He is no good! The NAACP is no good, it's communistic. I've been after him for six years. I finally was able to get him now!" Shortly afterward, I. B. Blumstein himself showed up with a security guard, who handcuffed her.

Meanwhile King sat still, calm, and lucid with the letter opener protruding from his chest. Spingarn tried to comfort him, holding his hand while they awaited the arrival of an ambulance. As they did so, a woman named Mrs. James Watson wanted to remove the blade (the elderly Mrs. Watson as well as a woman representing Mayor Wagner's office would later be placed under doctor's care due to stress from having witnessed the incident). But another witness who apparently had far more knowledge of the best way to handle such wounds insisted that no one touch it. While waiting, the stabbed King assured everyone, "That's all right! That's all right. Everything is going to be all right!"

At about 3:38 p.m. a phone at Harlem Hospital rang at the desk of Mrs. Constance Jennings. The person on the other end of the line told her that a man had been stabbed at Blumstein's Department Store and that an ambulance was needed right away. About a minute later Ronald Adams, a Harlem Hospital ambulance driver, and Mrs. Russie Lee, a licensed practical nurse, sped down Seventh Avenue to Blumstein's. Neither was yet aware that their patient was Martin Luther King. Upon arriving, Mrs. Lee, who had been a nurse for twelve years, looked at the letter opener protruding from the seated King's chest. Calmly, just as the woman before her had done, she warned everyone surrounding King not to touch the blade because she knew that if the blade were pulled out, it could mean instant death.

Lee then ordered Adams to bring the ambulance around to the rear of the department store, on 124th Street. Meanwhile she and a police officer moved King, still sitting in the chair, to the back of the store. When the ambulance arrived, Mrs. Lee saw to it that King was carefully placed on his back. Adams then sprang into the driver's seat. Lee got into the back next to King, who was fully conscious as Lee instructed him not to touch the letter opener. Without speaking, King did as he was told.

A few minutes before King's arrival, Ruth Richards, an RN, was told the ambulance was on its way back to the hospital with King. She couldn't believe what she was hearing. Even though she suspected the person on the other end of the line was kidding, she sprang into action. With the aid of two other RNs she began setting up blood plasma and preparing for what was called an emergency "cut down," to save Martin Luther King, Jr. At 4:06 P.M., King was brought into the hospital, where Mrs. Jennings registered his name into the emergency room log.

why did they take king to harlem hospital?

BY SEPTEMBER 1958, Charles Felton, a first-year resident at Harlem Hospital, felt lucky. He realized that the Negro medical universe was small, and for the most part segregated. The majority of Negro physicians and surgeons were excluded from most major medical centers, including those within New York City. Most received their M.D.'s from Howard University School of Medicine in Washington, D.C., or Meharry Medical College in Nashville, Tennessee. Then the bulk of them spent a year interning at one of a handful of hospitals: Freedman's, the teaching hospital of Howard University's medical school; George W. Hubbard, the teaching hospital of Meharry; or Harlem Hospital; Homer G. Phillips Hospital in St. Louis; Kate B. Reynolds Hospital in Winston-Salem, North Carolina; Lincoln Hospital in Durham,

North Carolina; Flint-Goodrich Hospital in New Orleans; Provident Hospital in Chicago; or John A. Andrew Memorial Hospital in Tuskegee, Alabama. Residency training in the specialties was another matter. For most of the approximately 175 Negroes receiving M.D.'s every year across the country by the late 1950s, the choice was either Freedman's, Harlem Hospital, Homer G. Phillips, Hubbard, or nothing at all. Felton was lucky enough to obtain one of these training slots. In September 1958, he was a first-year resident in Internal Medicine at Harlem Hospital.

Light brown in complexion, Charles was a native of New Orleans, where he graduated from Xavier University. Then for medical school he didn't attend Howard or Meharry or any other American school. Instead he traveled overseas to the University of Geneva, in Switzerland. When he shopped around for internships to apply for back home in the U.S., Harlem Hospital was on the top of his list.

With approximately nine hundred beds, it was the largest hospital in the country training Negro M.D.'s. At the same time, though, this medical center to which the stabbed King had been rushed suffered from the plight of most big municipal hospitals. At the beginning of the twentieth century almost all such facilities in New York City had been alms houses, meaning large charity sanitariums for the poor. They featured large open wards, often outdated equipment, overcrowding, and did their best to maintain decent sanitary conditions on strained budgets. All of this was true of Harlem Hospital, even as it employed more people than any other enterprise in Harlem. On an average day eleven babies were born on its maternity ward, while four persons on other wards saw their last days. At the same time, the hospital suffered from the same staffing shortages, low pay, and tensions between personnel common at municipal hospitals. And in the fall through the winter months, due to being located in a community with a tremendous number of poor residents, the census increased by as many as two hundred to three hundred patients, necessitating that beds be placed in the hallways and along the corridors, causing a person to encounter the sick even as he stepped off the elevators.

Yet as a place to gain experience treating the sickest of patients, you couldn't beat large municipal hospitals. Bellevue was the largest in New York City, and by 1958 the largest hospital in the nation. So coveted were its wards for the variety of cases seen on them that the three most prestigious medical schools in the city had services there. Harlem Hospital was considered an excellent place in which to obtain experience too, though as yet it had no affiliation with a medical school. The hospital had been founded in 1887 in the days when the community was all Caucasian. It didn't integrate its medical staff until 1925. And even as late as 1958 most of its departments were still run by Caucasians, though by then Negroes made up most of its interns and residents. The hospital also had a healthy share of foreign-born trainees. Among them were Charles's Japanese wife, Hiroko, a resident in Obstetrics and Gynecology. On Saturday afternoon September 20th, Charles and Hiroko had just finished their shifts and were about to join two of their friends for lunch when Charles was

called back into the hospital. He was told that as a first-year resident in Internal Medicine he was needed to assess an important
patient who had just been brought into the emergency room with
a stab wound.

Felton made his way to the emergency room, only to see Martin
Luther King, Jr., lying on a gurney with a letter opener protruding from the middle of his chest. The very surprised Felton introduced himself to King and reassured him. Then he listened to
King's heartbeat and breathing. Everything seemed stable. He
took an EKG. Again, everything seemed as close to normal as
could be under the circumstances. As Felton completed his examination of King, a team of emergency room nurses, surgeons, and
surgical residents raced into action and began preparing King for
the emergency "cut down," meaning emergency surgery. His mission accomplished, Felton was now free to spend the rest of his
day with his wife and their two friends. As he joined them, the
emergency room began filling up with reporters, onlookers, and
important people, such as Arthur Spingarn, A. Phillip Randolph,
and aides to Mayor Wagner. It was as if the president of the United
States had been brought in.

Governor Harriman was participating in a parade down Fifth
Avenue when he was notified that King had been stabbed. He
returned to his Upper East Side home and consulted with his
aides, becoming extremely worried. This being an election year,
any kind of negative publicity with regard to a celebrity could
affect the outcome of the vote in November. Suppose King died on
his watch? thought Harriman. People would spend time second-

guessing, maybe to the point of wondering why the governor had-n't insisted on better security to accompany King on his visit. And why had they taken such an important figure to Harlem Hospital anyway? Why not Mount Sinai or Columbia-Presbyterian?

When he was notified of the stabbing, Rockefeller wasn't in the city at all. Right after the Friday political rally in Harlem he made his way to nearby White Plains, just north of the city, for an appearance at a benefit for the George Washington Carver Community Center to shake hands with guests. Then, during the actual day of the stab-bing, he made his way to Albany, the state capital, over one hundred miles away, for another campaign appearance. Upon hearing of the crisis, he issued a statement expressing shock and prayers for King. But he had no intention of making it back to New York City and over to Harlem Hospital.

Harriman and his entourage saw their opportunity to make hay with Negro voters (though by no means would they publicly express fear that the doctors at Harlem Hospital weren't up to the task of saving King). They would merely demonstrate the gover-nor's concern by rushing to King's side. They headed back uptown. When they arrived at Harlem Hospital, they demanded answers about who would be in charge of treating King. The nerv-ous first detail among the hospital staff was already trying to locate that man, Chief of Surgery, Dr. Aubré Maynard. But this being a Saturday, the task was a difficult one. Little did they know that Maynard, who had been practicing medicine in Harlem for thirty-two years, was sitting in the Plaza Movie Theater on 59th Street, completely oblivious to all that was going on outside the theater.

waiting for little napoleon

IF THERE WAS anything the doctors at Harlem Hospital were used to, it was responding to trauma emergencies. Being in the midst of a community so much of which was a ghetto, it wasn't uncommon for depressed and frustrated Negro men to take out their anger about the racial realities they confronted on each other. Someone had too much to drink and became overly sensitive about a joke. Or a man had too much to drink and got fresh with another man's woman, or became overly sensitive when another man said something to his woman. A fight broke out. There were weapons involved—a gun or a knife—and before you knew it, an ambulance just like the one that had picked up King from Blumstein's Department Store was rushing in the latest stabbing or gunshot victim to Harlem Hospital. This type of thing hap-

pened so often it was a staple of stereotypes regarding Negro communities and of jokes told about the usefulness of Harlem Hospital.
At one point residents at Mount Sinai Hospital came to Harlem
Hospital just to learn from the trauma cases. The only catch was that
by 1958, often Caucasian physicians had the attitude that the majority of physicians at the hospital (being Negro) didn't know the best
way to handle what came through their facility.

This attitude was nothing new. Even though New York was a
cosmopolitan city, Negro physicians in Harlem and in the rest of
the city had been dealing with the medical community's version
of racial prejudice for quite some time (and members of the medical profession tended to be more conservative than members of
other learned professions to begin with). For years it had been
almost impossible for them to get staff appointments in the city's
large, respected public hospitals. An appointment at a municipal
facility like Harlem Hospital was good for the experience. But as
was true at all city hospitals, you couldn't charge for your services.
Thus for the patients who paid you, in 1958, there were few other
facilities for Negro physicians to admit their patients. Notably
within Harlem, there was nearby Sydenham Hospital (which
opened its staff to Negro physicians in 1945), and for a time,
Mount Morris Park Hospital which, before going bankrupt, had
been run by a group of physicians inexperienced in management.
For several years running, the lot of the Negro physician in New
York City, and even in Harlem, had been a hard one, no matter
how skilled he or she happened to be. Thus, particularly among
those of the generation who trained prior to the 1930s, the impli-

cations of the nascent civil rights movement led to feelings of bitterness that they were in the twilight of their careers and would-
n't be able to benefit from the new day that was dawning. This
sentiment was about to have huge implications with regard to surgery on Martin Luther King, Jr.

For a long time the typical Negro physician in Harlem had been
used to the following: starting his day at seven or eight A.M., he'd go
to his office in the basement of a brownstone, for example, to see
patients who preferred going to the doctor just before going to work.
He'd stay and continue seeing other patients until noon. Then after
lunch, he'd examine patients once more from one to four P.M. Then
for his patients who couldn't take time off from jobs—those who
worked in Manhattan below 96th Street—he would have evening
hours from six to nine P.M., and stay until he examined the last
patient, meaning he might not finish until eleven P.M. He might
make house calls as well between afternoon and evening hours.
These patients were often people on public assistance who couldn't
make it to a municipal hospital clinic. Such patients would call a
central number downtown and the center would, in turn, call one of
the Harlem physicians who had signed up for such services. Then the
physician would go to the homes and treat the patients, receiving
three dollars per call from the city.

As for your private patient, if he or she became severely ill and you
were on the staff of Harlem Hospital and that patient had no problem going to a city hospital, you admitted her or him knowing you'd
receive no compensation for her treatment. If your patient preferred
going to a voluntary hospital whose staff you could not join because

it didn't admit Negro physicians, then you referred her to a physician who could admit her and hoped that the proximity to your office after she got well meant she would return to you for regular check-ups and treatment of illnesses that didn't require hospitalization. And when it came to getting paid for services rendered to your patients with such limited incomes, you never sent bills. The typical patient paid what he could. And if he missed paying you for a prior visit but the next time he came he could afford to pay for that visit, you didn't remind him of the previous visit he still owed you for. You just forgot about it. This had been the lot of the typical Negro physician in Harlem who trained prior to what was now a new era in medical education: the era of residency training programs in different specialties that took three or more years to complete. And the chief of surgery at Harlem Hospital whom everyone was now frantically searching for had trained in that earlier era. Yet for plenty of other reasons, Aubré de Lambert Maynard was a frustrated man. And a controversial one.

Charles Felton distinctly remembered what he had been told during his internship year when he rotated through the department of surgery for a three-month period. A senior resident insisted he was to stand up whenever Maynard entered the ward and always say good morning. He was to be dressed in not only the standard-issue white coat but a white dress shirt with tie, and white buck shoes. And he was to tell Dr. Maynard "Good morning," yet not expect him to reply. A reply would be too much for this short, dark-skinned man of regal West Indian bearing to make to a lowly intern. Of course, plenty of surgical-staff chiefs around the country were noted for the militarylike etiquette they expected their trainees to follow. But Maynard carried things a lot farther than this. Anyone who encountered him was immediately struck by an underlying bitterness emanating from him—a bitterness sometimes seen in talented, intelligent Negro men frustrated with the day-to-day conditions a Negro faced. It was a bitterness that easily turned into a facade of extreme arrogance around other Negroes, an arrogance that then turned into the need to impress in the presence of Caucasians of note in order to make it clear that this particular Negro stood head and shoulders above the rest.

Aubré Maynard spent most of his youth in his home country, Barbados (though he was born in British Guyana). It wasn't until the age of fourteen, when his father sent for him, that he moved to New York City. Upon arriving, he received his high school education in a setting where he grew used to being the only Negro among Caucasians in rigorous academic settings. At overwhelmingly Caucasian Townsend Harris High, one of the most challenging public high schools in the country (alma mater of luminaries such as Oliver Wendell Holmes), admission was gained only through exam. When Maynard first started attending, on the way home each day it became necessary for him to dodge Irish-American boys in the neighborhood intent on beating him up. Then he attended City College, where he majored in Physics in the era when the college was so academically well respected, it was known as "the poor Jewish man's Harvard." After that Maynard was the only Negro admitted to the class of 1926 at

Columbia University's College of Physicians and Surgeons. But he felt compelled to withdraw acceptance of the admission offer when told he would have to transfer to Howard University School of Medicine for his clinical years because Columbia's teaching hospital (Columbia-Presbyterian) wouldn't accept a Negro medical student on its wards. Maynard considered that an insult. He hadn't even applied to Howard or Meharry. After withdrawing his acceptance to Columbia he attended New York University School of Medicine instead. Upon graduating he became one of the four Negro interns to break the color barrier on the house staff of Harlem Hospital. And to top it off, he scored higher than any other applicant that year for an internship, since these were also the days when medical graduates from everywhere coveted an internship at Harlem Hospital.

And now, thirty-two years later, he was Chief of Surgery. But on the day of September 20th, no one could find him. As Harriman, Spingarn, other VIPs, and hospital staff members who would have never been present on a Saturday gathered in the public corridor of the surgical suite, King was prepped for the emergency procedure. Surgical resident Leo Maitland and the nurses on the ward completed the "cut down," connecting intravenous lines to him, taking his blood pressure, washing his chest, properly isolating the area for operation. King was wide awake, lucid, and calm. Maitland immediately contacted two chest specialists on staff. One was Emil Naclerio, an Italian American. The other was a talented young Negro who had just completed his training in Thoracic Surgery by the name of John W. V. Cordice.

Naclerio was in his home in the Bayside section of Queens, dressed in a tuxedo, about to go to a friend's wedding at the Waldorf Astoria Hotel. Now he would have to skip the wedding. Cordice, with his daughter in tow, was collecting his mail at the office he was trying to open for private practice in the town of Orange, New Jersey. As soon as he heard that King had been brought in with a stab wound to his chest, Cordice raced to his car, headed for the New Jersey Turnpike, entered New York City via the George Washington Bridge, and made his way to the hospital. Upon arriving, he began examining the X rays a radiology resident had taken. While he was doing so, Naclerio walked in. Then came Austrian-born anesthesiologist, Helen Mayer. All three had always been ready to respond to such emergencies without the involvement of Maynard. Such cases came in so often, they were routine. Cordice, Naclerio, Mayer, and the radiologist on duty continued examining the X rays. They revealed that the tip of the blade of the letter opener that Curry had plunged into King's chest was lodged right in the spot where the innominate artery cleaves off from the aorta, the primary blood vessel leading out of the heart.

Given King's vital signs, it was clear that he wasn't in any immediate danger. But suppose the blade moved? All it might take to get the tip to pierce the aorta was a mere cough. And, given the pressure of the blood coming out of the aorta, even a small pierce would quickly become a rip and King would hemorrhage to death before anything could be done to stop the bleeding.

The four doctors huddled together and thought about the situation further. Had this not been Martin Luther King, Jr., they

would have gone in and operated immediately. But staff members who watched as the emergency room began filling up with
spectators had been right. Suppose something unforeseen took
place? The operating room suite was now filling up with more
and more VIPs, including now eminent surgeons called in from
rival medical centers by Harriman's aides: Mount Sinai,
Columbia-Presbyterian, New York Hospital, and so on—the same
men who tended to look down upon the staff at Harlem Hospital,
where the Department of Surgery was the sole department run
by a Negro. Upon further discussion of the situation round-robin,
the three surgeons and anesthesiologist agreed that since King
was not in immediate danger—since he wasn't agitated and his
vital signs were stable, at least for now—it would be best to wait
until Maynard could be located. It would be best to wait, even
though they had their own problems with Maynard that extended
beyond his reputation and his tendency to berate underlings,
traits that had earned for him the nickname around the hospital
of Little Napoleon. Yet little did they know that once Maynard
arrived on the scene, he would see in the situation an opportunity
to make hay for Harlem Hospital and for himself, to elevate the
reputation of the hospital with embellishments regarding what
happened in the operating room, embellishments that would survive for years to come.

ELEVEN

roots

WHILE HE WAS completing his undergraduate medical training in the early 1940s at the very medical school Maynard attended, the same John W. V. Cordice who was about to play a crucial role in performing surgery on King had been told by an NYU medical faculty member about an alumnus of his race who had been a wonderful student at NYU and was now doing great things up at Harlem Hospital. Over and over he kept hearing about the work this graduate and other Negro physicians and surgeons on the staff up there were doing. Perhaps such stories reminded Cordice of his father, which was why upon graduating from NYU, rather than accept an internship at Bellevue, John was determined to train at Harlem Hospital. Maybe such stories explained why Cordice became determined to train with a surgical staff that included Aubré de Lambert Maynard.

John Cordice was a product of the renowned Negro bourgeoisie of Durham, North Carolina, where his father had also been a doctor. Durham's Negro bourgeoisie had founded the venerable North Carolina Mutual Life Insurance Company, the largest Negro-owned insurance company in America, as well as other thriving businesses. They had coerced the Duke tobacco family to donate the seed money to erect Lincoln Hospital for the Negro community. Cordice's father, a 1917 graduate of Howard University School of Medicine, was on staff. And to John he cut a dashing, noble figure. As noted earlier, in the days when his father began practicing medicine, formal specialized training in the various specialties hadn't been launched yet. A year of internship in a hospital was considered enough, then a physician hung out his shingle and gravitated toward whatever area of medicine interested her or him. Cordice's father volunteered for the U.S. Public Health Service. The country had just entered the First World War. He thought he would be sent to Europe. Instead, the elder Cordice was sent to the town of Aurora, North Carolina, along the state's Atlantic coast. Very shortly the great worldwide flu epidemic of 1918 struck and the senior Cordice was the only doctor in the area who knew an effective treatment for the disease. He treated people of all colors.

John was born in 1919. Stories of the influenza treatments administered by his father instilled within him a tremendous pride and self-confidence in his roots. When he was six, his father moved the family to Durham. As John grew up among the prosperous Negro bourgeoisie of Durham, his father made sure he saw as little of the ugliness of the predominantly Caucasian Durham as possible. He instilled within John the notion that he could do anything. Upon graduating from high school after the eleventh grade, John told his father that he wanted to attend college at Duke. Of course in those days this was impossible due to his race. His mother wanted him to attend Hampton Institute. By contrast, his father had no intention of exposing him any longer to the deprivations of the Jim Crow South. He recommended that John head for New York City and apply to Columbia University. "Don't worry about the cost," the senior Cordice told his son. "You just get up there and stay with your aunt and I'll pay for it."

The year was 1935. Sixteen-year-old John headed for the city with a principal interest in flying airplanes. It was the age of Charles Lindbergh, who was still a hugely popular American folk hero after making the first transatlantic flight in history in 1927 in his airplane *The Spirit of St. Louis*. Subsequently he married Anne Morrow Lindbergh, with whom he began embarking on pioneering flights to Latin America and Asia in their own Lockheed Sirius seaplane. The Lindberghs became "the first couple of the skies." Then they became even more exposed to the public due to the 1932 kidnapping and murder of their baby son, Charles junior. Every youth was still fascinated by Charles Lindbergh. As John headed for the New York City area, he was determined that one of the things he would do was meet Lindbergh.

To John, this couldn't possibly be an unrealizable dream. After all, one of his aunts lived in Englewood, New Jersey, just a hop, skip, and jump from New York City, but also just a hop, skip, and jump from the borough of Hopewell, New Jersey, where the Lindbergh family lived. His aunt was part of the relatively prosperous band of Negroes who worked in the homes of wealthy Caucasians in the area. They considered themselves cultivated. Like John's father, she was eager to shield John from the racial realities of the day as much as possible. But, at the same time, she was determined to compensate for them. With this in mind she set out to fulfill John's dream to the greatest extent possible.

"Come over here, John," she instructed him, after calling her sister's home in Brooklyn. "You said you wanted to meet Lindbergh? Well, I have a surprise for you."

Excitedly John made his way over to his aunt's house. She put him in her car, and headed for the Lindbergh home. John was certain he was finally going to get his chance. When they arrived, rather than go through the front door, they made their way to the back, to the servants' entrance, and were allowed inside. When they got there, his aunt told him, "John, I'd like you to meet someone special. This here is Mr. Lindbergh's cook." That was the surprise. John was meeting not Lindbergh himself, but the next best thing a Negro in that day and age could expect, *Lindbergh's cook*. "She acted as though she was trotting out Lindbergh himself," Cordice would recall sixty-five years later. "I never did let her know how disappointed I was."

This was the first really hard-hitting introduction John had to the limitations of race, the first splash of cold water in his face, just as other talented, determined Negroes like Aubré Maynard had also received in their young lives. There would soon be others.

As his father recommended, not long after arriving in the city, John made his way to the registrar's office at Columbia University. He asked the woman at the front desk about enrolling. She completely ignored him. John felt that the place had a cold ambiance. He asked the woman behind the desk, once more, whom he should see about enrolling. Finally, in a rude voice she informed him he had to make an appointment, then handed him a catalog. John headed for the subway with the catalog in hand, shocked by such treatment. He wondered if he really did belong at Columbia. It was the first time he really began doubting himself, the first time he faced all the insecurities drummed into a Negro's head.

When he returned to Brooklyn, he had a talk with his aunt's husband, who began informing him of other realities as well. He told his uncle that he wanted to be an aviator, or maybe an engineer. "Are you out of your mind?" replied his uncle. "This world isn't going to let a colored man be an engineer. You have an opportunity to be a doctor, to go back home and do something good. I think that's what you ought to do."

That fall, John took evening classes at a local high school for a semester to bolster his academic record, thinking that with a strong extra layer of education there was no way Columbia would turn him down. Then he applied to the college. He was told that it didn't admit students midyear. The registrar told him that, by contrast, NYU did admit students in the middle of the academic year and that if he wanted to, he could start classes at NYU and then reapply to Columbia as a transfer student for his sophomore year. John started classes at NYU and liked the place so much that he just forgot all about Columbia. And he took his uncle's advice; he took premed courses with the intention of following in his father's footsteps, becoming a doctor.

John went on to graduate from NYU, then attend NYU Medical School. He started in 1940. The following year the U.S. entered into World War II, so the academic schedule of his class was accelerated so that it graduated in December 1943, instead of May 1944. At the time he attended the medical school, there were only three Negro students, the other two being two years ahead of him. All three would frequently go up to Harlem Hospital to talk to the legendary Negro NYU medical alumnus named Aubré Maynard.

The following year a graduate of Meharry Medical College who would intern and do his residency training in surgery at Harlem Hospital would get to know Maynard, too. John Parker would work night and day at the hospital and hear about how important it was to be on your toes when Little Napoleon, the attending surgeon, came through; that, given the manner in which he enjoyed grilling you, it was best to stay away from him if you could. So during his internship, Parker strove to steer clear of Maynard. He was always dog-tired anyway. One day his wife got a line on a short vacation rental up at Oak Bluffs, the Negro resort community on Martha's Vineyard. She was eager to take her exhausted husband up there, along with her mother and father, who were visiting at the time. So finally Parker found the time and they went. Upon their arrival, his in-laws were eager to know who it was with the car with the New York plates who vacationed in a very nice cottage next door. So they made themselves nosy and introduced themselves to a nice, short, erudite, dark-skinned West Indian man, who told them he was a surgeon, and that he practiced at Harlem Hospital. They returned to their own cottage and told John they had met a surgeon next door who said he practiced at Harlem Hospital, and that his last name was Maynard. They told him that they told the man they had a son-in-law who was interning there, and that he guessed who they were referring to. After that, dread built up in Parker.

All that week he avoided going next door, or even in the direction of next door, until finally he realized that he had to say something. Parker could see Maynard sitting in the nice backyard of the next-door cottage reading newspapers, with a stack of surgical journals piled beside him. So he walked up to Maynard and introduced himself. "Ahhhh, Parker," replied Maynard. "I was wondering when you were going to make it over here." At that Maynard picked up one of the journals and said to him, "Tell me what you know about the problem discussed in the first case in here." From that day on, Parker's vacation was ruined.

Such behavior on the part of Maynard was displayed by at least one other Negro surgeon at the hospital, his predecessor as chief of the department, Louis T. Wright, the man who had successfully agitated for Negro staff to be appointed to the hospital in the first place. Wright was older than Maynard. He had attended Harvard Medical School as one of only two Negroes out of eighty-seven matriculants in the class of 1915. He graduated cum laude, ranking fourth in the class, but wasn't elected to Alpha Omega Alpha, the honorary medical society, because he had been blackballed by a Jewish student from Memphis. After his internship at Freedman's Hospital (where he published the first scientific paper ever from a Negro hospital, proving that, contrary to scientific opinion, the Schick test for the presence of diphtheria, was, indeed, valid for Negroes, even though their skin was dark), he returned to his hometown of Atlanta and began practicing medicine with his stepfather. In addition he helped launch a branch of a new civil rights organization with another young Atlantan, a life insurance salesman named Walter White. The two men were preparing for as many frustrated Atlantans as possible to meet with the new field secretary of the organization, who was coming through the city to try to convince them that agitating for Negro rights through the association he was now part of was better than sticking to the Booker T. Washington formula of gradualism. When James Weldon Johnson came though Atlanta and discovered how well White organized the group and how well he could speak publicly, he offered him a job as assistant field secretary of the NAACP, requiring that he move to New York City. White wasn't sure if that was the best thing for him to do. So he discussed the offer with Wright, who told him to go ahead and move to New York City because if he stayed in Atlanta, he'd stagnate.

Shortly after that Wright left too, unable to stomach Jim Crow any longer. He enlisted in the Army Medical Corps during World War I, where his entire battalion was gassed with phosgene, leaving him slightly debilitated with a lung disease that over time would turn into full-blown TB. After being discharged from the army, he headed to New York City, where he served as an assistant physician in a venereal disease clinic. At the same time he was appointed clinical assistant visiting surgeon on the staff of Harlem Hospital, meaning he could treat patients in the outpatient clinic but not the hospital itself. He would be the first Negro appointed to the staff, period. With the aid of Negro politicians and community leaders in Harlem, Wright agitated some more, organizing the Negro physicians in the community, who in 1925 sent telegrams at two o'clock in the morning to Mayor Jimmy Walker and other operatives in the Tammany Hall political machine, demanding that they be appointed to the staff inside the hospital. The bold move resulted in the appointment of the five Negroes, including Wright himself, to the staff of the hospital.

The following year, 1926, Aubré Maynard and three other Negroes joined the class of new interns inside the hospital. Almost in tandem Maynard and Wright began making strides inside the hospital. Though they were never close personal friends, they respected each other, one from the West Indies, the other from the Deep South, both stubbornly intent on rising above the insults meted out to Negroes in their day and proving that they were as good as their Caucasian counterparts. After finishing his two-year internship (often called a houseship in those days), Maynard obtained a junior position on the hospital staff. He and Wright both learned as much as they could from the surgical cases coming through, setting high standards for themselves and for the other Negro physicians. Three years later Wright was appointed a police surgeon for the city of New York, scoring higher on the exam than all but one other applicant for one of the positions (who bested him by less than a percentage point). With this post, in which he would agree to look the other way at the rampant corruption and abuse he became privy to, Wright was able to secure a steady income while making further strides at Harlem Hospital and organizing a surgical society for budding Negro surgeons. Maynard became one of the first to enthusiastically join the organization.

So stringent were both men in what they expected from other Negro physicians and surgeons that a debate soon raged regarding which Negro physicians and surgeons were qualified to join the hospital staff (or remain on staff) and which were not. By that time, Wright had been given the green light by the city hospital bureaucracy, as well as the predominantly Caucasian staff of Harlem Hospital itself, to virtually choose which Negroes would be appointed and which ones would receive internships. Soon Wright decided that certain Negro staff members had to go because in his opinion they didn't measure up. By 1932 the issue became so alienating that Wright's faction (including Maynard) was publicly denounced by opposing Negro physicians in the community, who marshaled the aide of Reverend Adam Clayton Powell, Jr., and began protesting at City Hall what Wright was doing to remove the Negro physicians on staff whom he didn't think belonged at the hospital. It would take a few years for the controversy to blow over.

Meanwhile Wright also became active in civil rights. By the early 1930s, Walter White succeeded James Weldon Johnson and became executive secretary of the NAACP. Remembering the feistiness of his fellow Atlanta native, he convinced him to join the NAACP board of directors, which Wright began chairing in 1936. Wright became a relentless fighter for national civil rights, as well as a stubborn opponent of government-organized segregation in the construction of medical facilities for Negroes. He also became personal physician to several notable Negro celebrities, including W.E.B. Du Bois, and a friend to people such as Bill "Bojangles" Robinson. Simultaneously he began making further strides in his field. In 1934 he became only the second Negro surgeon to be admitted to the American College of Surgeons. Four years later he became a diplomat of the newly organized American Board of Surgery. He also became a medical and surgical researcher, devising a plate for certain types of fractures of the femur. In 1938, *Life* magazine named him the most eminent Negro physician in the United States In 1943 Wright was named chairman of the Department of Surgery and, in subsequent years, headed a research team that supported numerous medical investigations in the use of newly created antibiotics. His Harlem Hospital team would be the first to use the drug Aureomycin in human beings.

John Cordice would be part of Wright's investigative team in the use of antibiotics. But he would never forget how difficult it was to get close to the man and even interview for a surgical residency after he returned from his stint in the army, which he had entered after completing his nine-month internship at Harlem Hospital. The year of his discharge was 1947. During his internship he had seen Wright intensely grill others aspiring for residency slots in surgery at the hospital. Most such candidates were unsuccessful in gaining a spot. Only a certain number were going to Negroes. By the early forties the hospital staff was still quite integrated, indeed, the most integrated of any in the country. And given the position Wright was in as a police surgeon for the city, he had to meet a certain quid pro quo, allowing a certain number of Caucasians into the surgical training program at the hospital (as Maynard would be after him, Wright was the sole Negro M.D. heading a department in the hospital).

So Cordice was anxious to obtain one of the positions. But the question was, How? Back home in Durham everyone was anxious to see him return. John wasn't sure he wanted to. There was one physician in the community who might be able to cajole Wright into granting him a residency slot. Clyde Donner had been the only other Negro in the class of 1915 at Harvard Medical School. After graduating, Donner married Martha Merrick, the daughter of one of the founders of North Carolina Mutual Life Insurance Company. This meant that Donner had married into wealth. He became vice president in charge of the medical department at the company, a position that only required him to review medical claims. He was well aware of what Wright was up to at Harlem Hospital, and Wright remembered him well, too. So Cordice returned home and told Donner of his interest in a surgical residency under Wright. Donner looked at him and wondered why that was necessary.

"Cordice, let me tell you something," he said. "You're out of your mind. What you need to do is come back here to Durham, work with your dad, and be somebody. You don't need to go up there [to Harlem hospital]. First of all, Louis is crazy as hell. All he's going to do is work you to death. And you'll get no credit for what you do. You'll be busy writing papers, and so on. You aren't going to go anywhere with that. I wouldn't recommend it. And not only that, [Louis] is sick you know. He has TB. First thing you know, you'll get it too. You know, your sister died of TB. You don't want to make that trip. Trust me."

These were still the days when after completing an internship, an M.D. could learn by doing. And both Cordice and Donner were aware of the keen competition among Negro medical graduates for the few surgical training slots available to them.

"How else am I going to get my surgical training?" asked John. "How am I going to pass my boards?"

"You don't need any damn boards," Donner replied. "That's for white folks."

Cordice ignored the advice and repeated to Donner that he absolutely had to obtain a residency training slot at Harlem Hospital. He begged Donner to put in a call to Wright. Reluctantly Donner told him he would see what he could do.

After returning to New York City upon his honorable discharge from the army, Cordice had begun working in the pathology lab up at Montefiore Hospital in the Bronx. It was April 1947. Residency training appointments in surgery started in July. So after heading to Durham to talk to Donner, John returned to the Bronx. A few weeks later he received a call from Dr. Wright's secretary at Harlem Hospital giving him an appointment to see Wright. Excitedly, Cordice made his way to the appointment. Though Wright had passed him by when Cordice was an intern, this was the first time he now viewed John as anything but another face in the Harlem Hospital crowd.

So now he entered Wright's office. After the requisite greetings, Wright told him to have a seat. Nervously Cordice did as instructed. Wright sat behind his desk, then looked at him directly. "You wanna work here?" he asked John.

"Of course I do," replied John.

"Well, I'll tell you something. If you come to work for me, you're going to work. This is not going to be child's play. And as for calling Clyde Donner to try to get an in with me— Clyde is lazy as hell. He wasted his Harvard education, went down to Durham and married some gal whose father founded North Carolina Mutual, and all he's been doing ever since is drinking Cognac and resting!"

All John felt he could say to that was, "Yes sir! Yes sir!"

A few weeks later Cordice received notification that he should report to Harlem Hospital on July 1st. Wright's secretary informed him that he wasn't getting a residency training slot. Instead he would be an emergency room fellow, a position for which he wouldn't be paid. But he would get room and board in the house staff quarters. And while working in the emergency room he would be competing with another guy for an actual residency training slot the following year. Cordice felt compelled to take the deal. He worked hard in the emergency room, and at the end of the year not only did he receive a residency appointment in the hospital, so did the guy he was competing with.

Upon becoming part of the surgical house staff, Cordice became part of Wright's team investigating the use of Aureomycin in humans. This was an interest Wright began developing largely because of his increasingly debilitated physical condition (due to the past ravages of TB), which made it difficult for him to continue performing surgery, necessitating that he sit as he operated, then that he leave the operating room altogether, unable to withstand anesthetic vapors any longer. Wright succeeded in distinguishing research as a respected branch of the hospital. Residents on staff like Cordice became part of a 1948 *Life* magazine feature spread, lauding Wright's team for what they were up to. John even wrote a paper on the use of Aureomycin in tubercular menthalnopathy. His paper was published in the prestigious *Yearbook of Surgery*, which in Cordice's view, made

Wright not as tough and "crazy" as Clyde Donner implied. John knew that there were many surgical department chiefs who would have taken complete credit for his research and published such a paper under their own names, giving him second or third credit. Such tactics were common not only in academic medicine but in academia, period. And the reasoning had to do with hierarchy, with being a good team player. As such, any discoveries or breakthrough progress made under the leadership of the person responsible for admitting you to the department or the company were supposed to be credited to the man or woman at the helm of the ship, so to speak.

So Cordice became part of the department. He conducted research, examined surgical cases, and soon began performing surgery. He also began observing the other man in the department with the reputation for uncompromising excellence—that fellow graduate of NYU's School of Medicine, Aubré de Lambert Maynard. Yet Cordice already had reservations about him. He had begun to feel that way while he was still an intern. One morning he was told that Maynard would be operating. The case involved a very wizened, well-respected old lady in the community who had abdominal cancer. Cordice scrubbed and observed as Maynard and his assistants opened her abdomen, only to see that the tumor was everywhere. Clearly her case was hopeless. There was nothing Maynard could do for her. John had been expecting to see in Maynard some indication of compassion for what lay before him—whether in his body language or in the way he addressed those assisting him—something to show that he was saddened by what he saw, the type of thing Cordice had observed in other surgeons at the hospital. But he observed the exact oppo-site. All Maynard did was suck in his teeth, make some sutures, and close the elderly woman back up without saying one word. John was shocked.

And now he was back at Harlem Hospital as a surgical resident. In 1952 Wright died of a heart attack at the age of sixty-two. The issue became who was going to succeed him as chairman of the department. What Cordice had observed about Maynard in the operating room that day in 1944 was among the many things that troubled other physicians and surgeons at the hospital about him. Yes, he was good at the theory of surgery. But there was that attitude, and the sense that he was a prima donna. The hospital board met in November 1952 to choose Wright's successor. Everyone was adamant that no matter how good Aubré Maynard was as a surgeon, he was not going to be chairman of the department. The board voted. They chose Dr. Ralph Young. Yet word had it that, knowing he was sick, Wright had already spoken to the director of the New York City Department of Hospitals about the man who should succeed him in the event of his untimely demise. Allegedly, he told Dr. Marcus Kogel, the Commissioner of Hospitals, that that man should be Aubré Maynard, even though throughout the time they knew each other, Wright and Maynard had never been pals, so to speak. Allegedly Wright thought his replacement should be Maynard pre-cisely because he was good. So after receiving the recommenda-tion of Harlem Hospital's board that Ralph Young be named the new chairman of the department, Kogel overruled the board and named Maynard chairman. The board insisted it wouldn't stand for

Maynard chairing the department. But Kogel held his ground and Maynard became chairman anyway.

John Cordice had just completed his training in general surgery. Before completing it, he had written another paper (this time regarding heart surgery) that was scheduled for publication. At the time of completion, Maynard was chief of the Division of Thoracic Surgery, which he had established in 1947 at the request of Wright. Upon receiving notification about its desire to publish the paper, Maynard instructed the journal that he, Aubré Maynard, was to receive first credit for the research. In fact, he had had absolutely nothing to do with the research. Of course, he was just following the usual procedure of plenty of department and division heads in academia. Yet, by then, Cordice was used to the fair treatment meted out by Wright. By contrast, not only was there no question in Maynard's mind that, as chief of the Division of Thoracic Surgery, his name should go first, there was even some doubt as to whose name should go second.

By then, Emil Naclerio was an attending in thoracic surgery. Naclerio had been added to the department in 1950, shortly after Helen Mayer was recruited as an expert anesthesiologist. Mayer had trained at Columbia-Presbyterian and the University of Chicago. She was an expert in endotracheal anesthesia and respiratory physiology and would establish the residency program in anesthesiology at the hospital. She recommended to Maynard that he recruit Naclerio, a thoracic surgeon educated at Marquette Medical School in Wisconsin. He had just completed his advanced training in bronchio-pulmonary and heart surgery in England. Upon his arrival, he delved into that subspecialty with brio, becoming the hospital's expert in that area, breaking traffic rules to reach the emergency cases that came in. So by 1951 the situation in the hospital was: Naclerio was now on staff as the enthusiastic new junior attending in thoracic surgery; John was a senior surgical resident; Maynard was chief of the division—a chief who, choosing to exercise his prerogative as the senior man in the division, did not come in for emergencies. And the other prerogative he chose to exercise was placing his name first on any paper describing breakthrough research that had been conducted in his division. So the issue at that point was, Should Naclerio's name go second on the paper describing research conducted by Cordice, even though most of the work had been done by the more junior Cordice?

Cordice began observing other things about Maynard. Yes, he was a competent surgeon. He really knew his theory due to his practice of reading up on the latest in the surgical journals. But in Cordice's opinion, Maynard couldn't improvise in the operating room. There were reasons for this. One was that, though he was board certified, still Maynard was of the generation of surgeons at the hospital who, in learning primarily by working on patients they elected to see, had virtually no *required experience* with most cases that came through the hospital. This was routine for surgeons who learned the craft in the early days of development of the specialty with only a year or two in hospital internships, far shorter than the five years of training that became standard once residencies were established. As a result, when the American Board of Surgery was established in 1937, the practical examination for board certification wasn't as stiff as it became ten to fifteen years down the road when more was known in the field and more procedures had been developed. Thus by the 1940s standards were stiffer even though formal surgical residencies were already well established due to the fact that at the typical big-city hospital the residency house staff learned by performing surgery on any and every case that came through the doors. At the same time, the more senior you were on staff at such a typical big-city teaching hospital, the less likely you were to come in and observe emergencies.

"By the time I became chief resident, most of the attendings didn't even want to scrub with me because I knew more than they did," recalls John Parker, who became Chief Resident in Surgery at Harlem Hospital in 1950. "And the senior attendings never came in for emergencies. I can't ever recall Maynard coming in for an emergency. I may be wrong on that. I'm just saying that I don't recall him coming in."

Cordice can't recall any such time either. But because of the typical pyramidal hierarchy of the big-city hospital, when it came to who was going to be chosen head of a division or department, the guys who had trained in the old days were still given priority over graduates of formal residency training programs. Yes, Maynard did make the effort to learn more than most of the other senior attendings at Harlem Hospital. And he kept up with the latest developments *in theory* only. In essence, he did more than the typical surgeon of his generation to know as much as he could possibly know.

And he did take some interest in Cordice. After finishing his residency, John tried to obtain advanced training in thoracic and cardiovascular surgery. It wasn't until two years later that this happened. With the help of Maynard and Dr. Peter M. Murray, a gynecologist at Harlem Hospital, he secured a fellowship under the direction of Harlem Hospital and Columbia-Presbyterian Hospital. Then the following year Cordice received another fellowship to study the same subspecialty in France. Upon his return, he was finally able to break the racial barrier and get two more years of formal training at Downstate University Medical Center in Brooklyn.

With this experience under his belt, by 1958, when he finished his formal training, Cordice's knowledge of cardiovascular and thoracic surgery was far superior to Maynard's. And the same was true for Naclerio. Both men had been having fun in the operating room, often all day and all night. One night both were on call when a stab wound to the neck came into the emergency room (a very dangerous injury because it involves the trachea and the carotid artery). At the same time, a heart wound came in. The two surgeons had to decide which case to operate on first. They noticed that the patient with the heart wound had some blood pressure. So they tamponated it (meaning that they stopped the bleeding, rendering the case far less dangerous than the neck wound). The next day Cordice told Maynard about the two cases. Maynard asked which they operated on first, in effect, revealing his lack of knowledge of which was more urgent. Cordice told him they did the neck wound first because they suspected that the patient had a carotid injury that might bleed out. As time went on, these exchanges between Cordice and Maynard grew more and more frequent. Like Naclerio, he became vital to the division's success.

Yet Little Napoleon had a difficult time coming to terms with this. That kind of thing was hardly unusual in the world of academic medicine. The younger guys were always becoming the victims of jealousy on the part of their elders. When Cordice returned to Harlem Hospital in 1958 as a junior attending, Maynard began limiting his horizons. One day the secretary of the prestigious New York Surgical Society, a surgeon named Jerry Lord, became aware of how good Cordice was in the operating room because after finishing his training, Cordice was also admitted to the staff of Columbus Hospital on 18th Street, where Lord was also on staff. Aubré Maynard was only the second Negro to be invited to join the society (the first had been Wright). After discovering how good Cordice was, and knowing he was on the staff of Harlem Hospital, Lord began wondering why Maynard hadn't nominated him for the surgical society. A surgeon had to have three society members nominate him. And usually the chief of his department was one of them. So Lord asked Cordice about this. John responded that he didn't know why Maynard hadn't nominated him. One day at a surgical society meeting, Lord confronted Maynard on the issue.

"How dare you tell me whom I should recommend for nomination to the surgical society!" Maynard is said to have replied. A month later he walked up to Cordice and told him he wasn't ready to be nominated for the New York Surgical Society.

On September 20, 1958, this was the man Cordice, Naclerio, Mayer, and Leo Maitland, Chief Resident of Surgery, waited for as Martin Luther King, Jr., lay on an operating room gurney awaiting removal of the letter opener that Izola Curry had plunged into his chest. Though Maynard had established the Division of Thoracic Surgery, Naclerio and Cordice knew more about what to do. Still, Maynard was now chairman of the entire department and accountable for anything that went wrong. The two surgeons decided what to do in light of this. They would wait for his arrival before opening King's chest. Then, when it was time to actually remove the letter opener, they would leave that to Maynard in what would amount to a ceremonial gesture of respect for their chairman. Little did they know this wouldn't be the story the rest of the world would hear.

saving king

WORD OF WHAT happened to King made its way onto the newswires, spreading across the country, and causing Southern racists to laugh out loud with glee that "one of his own people" had apparently done in King. J. B. White, a Bainbridge, Georgia, coal dealer, immediately began taking up a collection among friends to send to Curry as a legal defense fund. After Curry was handed over to police, she was taken to Harlem Hospital, where the prostrate King identified her as his assailant. Upon seeing King, Curry once again spewed epithets against Negro preachers, accusing King of causing her to lapse in her Catholicism. After her identity was confirmed, she was driven to the local 123rd Street Precinct for booking on charges of felonious assault, then temporarily locked up until being transferred to the East 67th Street stationhouse, which had facilities for keeping women.

Meanwhile, as the hunt for Maynard continued, a crowd of thousands gathered in front of the hospital. About forty people walked into the emergency room and offered to give blood to save King. In an inner operating suite, Governor Harriman comforted King, who had been moved away from the notables who were gathering in the outer area of the operating suite. The surgeons from Mount Sinai, Columbia-Presbyterian, Bellevue, and New York Hospital remained in the outer suite discussing with one another what they would do in the same situation, talking with staff members who wouldn't be part of the operating team, while Cordice, Naclerio, Maitland, and Mayer remained inside the inner sanctum waiting to see if Maynard would be found. Over an hour had passed and still there was no sign of him. Using his authority, the governor could have had King moved to another medical center. But the surgeons in the suite convinced him that this wouldn't be wise.

Meanwhile the French film that Maynard had been watching at the Plaza Theater on 59th Street—*La Parisienne*, starring Bridgette Bardot—was finally over. Afterward, on this Saturday he was scheduled to make rounds at another hospital where he was on staff, a private facility named Manhattan General. Maynard retrieved his car from a parking garage and made his way there. Upon walking into the hospital lobby, the administrator of Manhattan General rushed up and told him he had to make his way to Harlem Hospital because a person of great importance had been rushed in with a stab wound to his chest (apparently he avoided telling Maynard who it was so as to ensure Maynard wouldn't become nervous while making his way back to the hospital).

Maynard drove north up the FDR Drive along the banks of the East River, turning off at 135th Street. From there it was a straight shot to the hospital. He arrived to a front entrance so packed with onlookers that he couldn't get through. He informed the police officers present who he was and told them to maintain crowd control. They formed a flying wedge and quickly got him through the crowd while telling him that the patient awaiting his arrival was Martin Luther King, Jr. Upon reaching the operating suite, Maynard waded through the crowd of notables into the inner operating sanctum, only to confront the stern countenance of Governor Harriman sitting on a stretcher flanked by his security men.

"Where have you been?" Harriman asked him with annoyance in his voice. Not far away King was lying on a stretcher, silent, prepared for surgery, with his eyes closed, the letter opener protruding from his chest. Maynard assured the governor that everything was under control, that while he was being located, King hadn't been neglected. After this he made a preliminary examination of King and assured him that everything would be fine. Then he went into a room and consulted Cordice, Naclerio, Mayer, and Maitland, who brought him up to speed on the situation. Maynard greenlighted the surgical approach they had decided to take, then he returned to the outer part of the operating suite and talked to the surgeons from other hospitals as well as to reporters. The other surgeons immediately began offering their advice on how to proceed. Though like the rest of the staff he was miffed at this intrusion, Maynard remained calm and reiterated to all present that this was a Harlem Hospital case and that his team was accustomed to this type of trauma. Then he invited some of the more notable surgeons to scrub and observe the operation.

While Maynard was doing this, Naclerio, Cordice, Maitland, and Mayer went ahead and scrubbed, administered the anesthesia to King, and opened his right chest the way they had opened numerous other chests before King's. They made what was called a curving intercostal condular (spangaro) incision, which didn't require removal of any of King's ribs, just an incision between the third and fourth interspace between the ribs. This incision was extended by a second one that would leave King with a cross-shaped scar he would joke about for the rest of his life (though to others it would appear to be shaped more like the letter T). Then they ligated the right internal mammary artery, inserted a rib spreader, spread the area between the third and fourth intercostal space, and viewed the aorta and vessels branching off of it. The entire opening procedure took about ten minutes. At that point they couldn't see the tip of the knife point, but they could feel it with their fingers coming through the inside of the manubrium, the top bone of the sternum, located in the middle of the chest where the left and right sides of the rib cage meet. They marveled at the strength of Curry to plunge a letter opener through this thick bone designed to protect the heart and aorta. Just as they expected, the tip of the letter opener was lying right at the point where the innominate artery branches off from the aorta. It was lying right in the crotch, close enough that the infamous line King would utter many times afterward could have been true: Had he sneezed violently enough, there's a good chance he would have drowned in his own blood.

By now Maynard had scrubbed and entered the surgical field. Naclerio and Cordice demonstrated to him what they had before them. With his gloved hand, Maynard grabbed the protruding unsterile gauze-covered blade of the letter opener, attempting to extricate it from King's chest. But the gauze slipped off and the blade knicked Maynard's glove. It was torn. So Maynard had to leave the surgical field to change gloves. While he did so, Naclerio, Cordice, and Maitland looked around at the adjacent tissues to ensure that nothing more was damaged than what they could already see. Maynard returned wearing new gloves. At that point Cordice took what was called a Kocher clamp—a sturdy surgical clamp with twin jaws—and placed it on the unsterile protruding section of the blade of the letter opener, which had been covered once more with gauze. Then he handed it to Maynard, telling him, "Look, if you're going to pull on it, pull on it with this."

Maynard appeared a bit flustered. He took the Kocher clamp off. Calmly, Cordice took a second clamp and placed it around the blade and invited Maynard to pull the blade out of King's chest. Either Cordice or Naclerio could have easily done it. Maynard removed the clamp again. Cordice placed a third Kocher clamp around the blade. By now he and Naclerio had grown impatient with Maynard's lack of recognition that they were trying their best to be respectful to the chairman of their department, whom they had waited for so patiently, this man who wasn't as skilled at thoracic surgery as they were. After placing this third clamp around the blade, both Naclerio and Cordice said, "Go on, take it out." Maynard began tugging on the blade. Finally, with a fair amount of effort it came out.

After this, Maynard walked outside to discuss the success of the operation with the governor and reporters, leaving Cordice, Maitland, and Naclerio to close King's chest. It was determined that about six centimeters of the blade had invaded the superior mediastinal compartment covering the innominate artery, aorta and other blood vessels, and the vital organs. This meant that the mediastinal tissue was contaminated. But experience taught Cordice, Maitland and Naclerio that all they needed to do was allow the body to take care of correcting the contamination on its own. So they closed the chest properly. This fact would be a very important one in light of the false description of the operation given by Maynard. At the press conference held in the office of the superintendent of the hospital after the entire operation was over—with Maynard, Cordice, Naclerio, and Dr. Farrow Allen present (Allen had scrubbed but did not participate in the operation)—Maynard gave the clear impression that he had been in command of the entire operation from start to finish. He told the reporters that a portion of King's second rib and part of his breastplate (sternum) had had to be removed. He said that the blade had cut a number of blood vessels, and that its location caused "considerable difficulty."

Of course, most of this was a fabrication. But Cordice, Naclerio, Maitland, and Allen said nothing. A few days later Maynard gave a further fabrication of what had happened to a reporter for the *Amsterdam News*. He would tell James Hicks that rather than pulling out the blade, it had been "pushed up from below." Several years later in a book he would write about his experience as a

Harlem Hospital surgeon, Maynard would similarly fabricate details. Contrary to what Maynard stated on the day of the operation and wrote later, no removal of any portion of any of King's ribs took place. This wasn't necessary. And no vital blood vessels had been severed. In providing his written description of the operation, Maynard would also claim that *he* left a "cluster of Pemrose drains"—which constituted rubber tubes allowing drainage to the outside—in the area of the superior mediastinum of King's chest. He would describe this procedure as an "on-the-spot innovative technique" that he came up with. He would claim that on the third postoperative day, he called in Dr. Robert Wylie, Chief of Thoracic Surgery at Columbia University College of Physicians and Surgeons, to examine the postoperative progress of King. And that upon examining King's right chest, Wylie "seemed particularly impressed with my innovative prophylactic drainage of the superior mediastinum" (the alleged cluster of Pemrose drains). In fact, not only had Maynard left the patient to be closed by the other surgeons but to do what he described, leaving Pemrose drains in the chest, would have been the worst possible thing that could have been done because leaving such tubes there would have left the mediastinum open to contamination.

Maynard wrote other falsehoods about the operation. For instance, he would claim that a hammer and chisel were used to remove bits of the breastbone that the blade had penetrated, in order to loosen the area around the blade. And then, rather than pushing out the blade, as he allegedly told Hicks, he later wrote that the blade was grabbed and, using a seesaw motion, loosened and extricated. Again, as described earlier, this was not done, just as his description to Hicks of how the blade was removed was false too. Using a hammer and chisel to chip away bits of the sternum would have been too dangerous. And to use a seesaw motion to remove the blade also would have been too dangerous, given the fact that the blade was so close to the aorta and the innominate artery. To try to remove it that way would have risked tearing the aorta or innominate artery, causing the massive hemorrhaging everyone feared.

Yet Maynard successfully fabricated not only his level of involvement in the operation on King, but the details of what took place. And accounts giving him a larger role in the operation than he deserves would become part of history. For years to come, even though so many colleagues hated him, out of respect for Maynard's position as Chairman of the Department of Surgery, no one felt compelled to correct the record.

convalescence

THE FOLLOWING DAY King's wife, Coretta, as well as his mother, brother, and father arrived at the hospital. While the others flew in from Montgomery and Atlanta, Martin senior arrived from the Midwest, where church work had taken him. They were all joined later by Ralph Abernathy and others. When they reached the hospital, the staff told them they could sit beside King and visit two at a time. Now he had security in the form of two New York City police officers on either side of the door to his room. King lay in his bed, his right chest bandaged from the shoulder down. An oxygen tube entered his left nostril, taped to his face, the tape forming a wishbone from his forehead to the bottom of his eyes. Photos of Emil Naclerio checking on him at bedside would be splashed across newspapers around the world. They would become part of the stock photos of the King oeuvre through the years, paged through whenever people considered his life in photo-essay collections.

Plenty of others would stop by his bedside. Governor Harriman returned. Ever worried about the Negro vote in the race against Rockefeller (given that the voting would take place in a little more than a month), doing his best to make the most out of a show of public concern, the governor posed for a public photo opportunity with Coretta, Abernathy, and M. L. King, Sr., and his wife.

Charles Felton would return to visit King too. He brought along another resident in the hospital named Bob Wilson, who had been a medical student at Boston University and roomed with King while King studied theology there. Periodically during King's stay they'd go up and Wilson and King would reminisce about their days in Boston. King also gave a few media interviews. In one, a reporter from the *Amsterdam News* asked him the proverbial questions leaders like him were expected to answer about what Negroes must do next. Dutifully, referring to the hot-button issue of school integration, King replied, "Our next stop is to implement what the courts have written on the books. If we Negroes do not implement the court's decision, [that decision] will prove meaningless."

Meanwhile after her arraignment, Izola Curry was transferred to Bellevue Hospital by magistrate Vincent P. Rao, for the purpose of undergoing a battery of mental tests. While sitting in her room at the mental hospital, she smoked cigarettes and read her mail. Curry was the recipient of hundreds of letters, some critical of what she had done, others commending her. In addition she received envelopes containing donations from racists for her

"legal defense fund." For some reason the donations were particularly plentiful from King's home state of Georgia. There was
$12.13 from a group in the town of Crottersville, calling itself "the
people of Georgia"; she received a $15 donation from a magistrate
in the town of College Park who obviously disagreed with the
actions of his New York counterpart in sending Curry to Bellevue;
and there were two $5 donations from a White Citizens Council
group in the town of Bainbridge. The coal dealer J. B. White of that
town would claim to have sent her "a substantial amount."

Speaking to a reporter about what he and six of his friends had
done, White described how they were all sitting around in a drug-
store when they heard the news. He would tell of how they found the
stabbing particularly hilarious because it had taken place in the "cra-
dle of integration." White opined that there were some good Negroes
who knew their place and that their ranks included Curry. Yet he
would also say that the races weren't meant to mix, that if God had
meant that to be the case, he would have made everyone the same
color. Clearly he had no understanding of what the deranged Curry
had stated regarding her personal philosophy, which was that Negroes
should appeal directly to the federal government for their civil rights,
bypassing Negro preachers and organizations such as the NAACP.

King continued convalescing in Harlem Hospital, being
checked on by Naclerio, Cordice, and Maynard. Coretta and the
rest of his family continued to visit him. They also made public
displays of concern for the rest of the patients in the hospital. On
one of those days, as photographers trouped along, Coretta and
her father-in-law donated some of the flowers King junior
received to children on the Pediatric ward.

As they did so, the civil rights rival who treaded lightly with King, who hadn't appeared with him at the Friday night rally, also showed his concern. Roy Wilkins was on a trip to Long Island on the Saturday afternoon King was stabbed. When he returned to the city and heard news of the crisis, Wilkins joined the other luminaries at the hospital waiting for word of the outcome of surgery. Four days later he spoke with Coretta on the phone, assuring her that of all the hospitals in the world, her husband was in the best one he could be in for the treatment of knife wounds and pneumonia. The following day he wrote King a letter offering whatever help he needed while recovering from the stabbing.

A week after surgery, King held a formal press conference while still in the hospital. He was asked what he thought of Curry; did he believe that she could have been part of a conspiracy by racists to assassinate him, specifically designing the execution to be performed by "one of his own," since he wouldn't expect that? "I have no knowledge of that," King replied. "But it is a possibility. Even if she is unbalanced, an unbalanced person can be used by balanced people."

On the fourteenth postoperative day King was released from the hospital. But he had to remain in the city for approximately two more weeks. He would stay at the home of Reverend Sandy Ray, pastor of Cornerstone Baptist Church in Brooklyn (Ray was an old friend of Martin senior). Upon walking out of the hospital, King was greeted by a throng of about five hundred people, whom he spoke to informally. Then he was whisked off. A few days later he would appear before a grand jury along with witnesses to the stabbing, to recount what had happened. Their testimony, as well as the mental health tests performed on Curry, would result in her being declared mentally unfit to walk the streets and confinement to a state psychiatric facility for several years.

As for the gubernatorial election that took place six weeks after the stabbing, the momentum favored Rockefeller until the final week and a half, when Democratic heavyweights finally rallied to Harriman's support. Former President Harry Truman, a Democrat, released an indignant statement taking issue with Rockefeller's implication that he was supporting him. Former First Lady Eleanor Roosevelt, who had been bitter about the outcome of the state convention nominating Frank Hogan for senator, put that feeling aside and denounced Rockefeller's running mate as entirely too conservative. And Harlem's most powerful politician, who had been conspicuously absent during the King stabbing, and whom Republicans had tried to get to endorse Rockefeller, finally weighed in in favor of Harriman.

Democrat Adam Clayton Powell, Jr., had famously crossed party lines in 1956 and endorsed Eisenhower for president. So it was not outside the realm of possibility that he would endorse the more liberal Rockefeller two years later for governor. Ever the pragmatic wheeler-dealer, Powell made peace with Tammany Hall leader Carmine De Sapio, agreeing to back Harriman in exchange for De Sapio backing his effort to become the first Afro-American chairman of a congressional committee. Once the deal was in place, Powell proceeded to lash out against Rockefeller, calling his family's infamous support for Negro colleges nothing more than an effort to sustain "Jim Crow colleges" and buy their way into respectability. This, Powell opined, contrasted with the Rockefeller family's lack of support for Negro civil rights. He claimed that in that regard their record was meager, as evidenced by their virtual lack of financial support to the NAACP.

Then Powell leveled the charge that an important Republican party operative had approached him and offered him "a bundle" in an effort to get him to back Rockefeller. Charles Willis, the man who allegedly did this, had been a very important go-between in securing Powell's endorsement of Eisenhower in 1956. Willis denied the bribery accusation, and in any case, had left no paper trail. Besides that, there was no verifiable connection between Rockefeller and Willis.

Yet the accusations leveled by Powell severely damaged Rockefeller in the minds of Negro voters. On two consecutive nights just before the election, Rockefeller struck back before Harlem audiences. He denied the allegation of bribery, and proudly pointed out that his family's record of philanthropy amounted to a total of $55 million donated to "aid Negro education." And as for their support of current efforts on the part of Negroes to secure their civil rights, Rockefeller stated his family had been contributors to the NAACP since 1928. And he cited his personal donations to the potent NAACP legal defense fund whose work was responsible for catalyzing the U.S. Supreme Court decisions affecting schools in Little Rock. Personally, Rockefeller had contributed $5,000 to the fund in 1951 and 1956. He cited Thurgood Marshall himself as someone who could confirm this (which Marshall did).

But the damage had been done. The Rockefellers staged a gala rally on Seventh Avenue in Harlem just a couple of weeks before the election, starring Cab Calloway, Count Basie, and comedian Nipsy Russell, all of whom the crowd loved and applauded. But when Rockefeller and his family and running mate took the stage, their applause was anemic. On the first Tuesday in November, Averell Harriman, the same man who grew nervous over King being taken to Harlem Hospital, won Harlem and the rest of the Negro vote. Yet he lost the general election to Rockefeller by more than half a million votes.

FOURTEEN

subsequent fates

UPON LEAVING New York City and returning to the Deep South,
Martin Luther King, Jr., of course, would go on to accomplish all that
he subsequently became known for: civil rights campaigns in places
such as Albany, Georgia; Birmingham, Alabama; Selma, Alabama,
and so forth, until that fateful day in Memphis in April 1968. As for the
hospital in Harlem briefly cast into the limelight, subsequent years
would not prove to be so advantageous. As the fifties came to an end,
hospitals across the country experienced a shortage of physicians,
resulting in a opening of the floodgates to foreign medical graduates.
By 1960, one-third of all hospital staff members in the country were
graduates of medical schools in places other than the United States or
Canada. The figure for New York City was even higher: 48 percent.
And Harlem Hospital, of course, was hardly immune. Foreign medical graduates began composing most of the house staff since city

hospitals were less desirable than voluntary and university-based hospitals, due to the lower salary and quality of services provided to their interns and residents. The only department that continued to attract plenty of U.S. graduates was Maynard's department: Surgery.

A result of this barely regulated entry of so many foreign medical graduates into the United States was a diminished quality of patient care at numerous hospitals across the country. Too many of the foreign medical graduates didn't have the basic skills necessary for good patient care. By 1960, the American medical establishment decided to require a test that all foreign medical graduates had to pass. When twenty-three interns at Harlem Hospital failed the exam, it caused an immediate controversy in the press. The only department that had no foreign medical graduates fail was Surgery. Something had to be done.

That same year, in the interest of saving city hospitals from a reduced quality of medical care, Dr. Willard Rappleye, dean of the medical school at Columbia, came up with a plan both to pay attending physicians to staff city hospitals full-time and to affiliate every city hospital with a medical school. The following year, Dr. Ray E. Trussel, commissioner of the city's Department of Hospitals, recommended to Columbia's medical school that it change its city hospital affiliation from Bellevue to Harlem Hospital, which was much closer. The recommendation would cause a tremendous uproar. One reason was because in the world of medicine there had always been a wide gulf between academic physicians and physicians in private practice. In the case of Harlem Hospital this gulf would be further exacerbated by race. Afro-American physicians at Harlem Hospital hardly welcomed the prospect of oversight from a medical school such as Columbia, one of the most prestigious in the entire country and thus one where the faculty tended to look down on physicians from elsewhere in the city (with the exception of those affiliated with Cornell's medical school). By the same token, plenty of Columbia faculty members hardly welcomed the prospect of taking under their wing an essentially Afro-American hospital in Harlem. The faculty member who was particularly nasty in that regard would prove to be Dr. Stanley E. Bradley, Chairman of the Department of Internal Medicine.

This department was the one weak spot at Harlem Hospital. The department heads and administrators decided that the best way to rectify the weakness now that the attending staff would be paid would be to recruit a good Afro-American specialist in internal medicine. Yet every single one of the prospects interviewed and presented to Columbia as a new prospective head of the department—the most talented Afro-American physicians in the area—was rebuffed by Columbia. A Caucasian physician was chosen instead. Even after that, the chairman of Columbia's Department of Internal Medicine refused to place Harlem Hospital's department under his jurisdiction. It was placed instead under the supervision of Columbia's Department of Administrative Medicine. The situation in the department wouldn't improve until 1968, when Gerald Thompson, an Afro-American, was appointed Chief of Internal Medicine at Harlem Hospital. By that time Aubré Maynard had reached mandatory retirement age and was no longer Chairman of the Department of Surgery.

In 1969, an entirely new Harlem Hospital was opened at the corner of Lenox Avenue and 135th Street, still affiliated with Columbia, an affiliation that continues to this day, though most of the attendings and house staff remain predominantly non-Caucasian.

epilogue

FOR ONE WEEK in September 1958 the lives of King, Harriman, Rockefeller, Curry, Michaeux, Maynard, Cordice, and others intersected in a manner that exposed human dynamics on many different levels. When King arrived in New York City, he understood the importance of the people of Harlem to the nascent struggle he was leading in the South, and the importance of broadcasting his message to the nation as a whole through his new book and through speeches. To do so would help raise much-needed funds for the work ahead. No doubt he understood the quid pro quo he was part of, involving the gubernatorial contest between Rockefeller and Harriman. With his popularity King could draw Negro voters for the two candidates to speak to while demonstrating their support for the exciting developments taking place in the South. What the presence of Rockefeller and Harriman, in turn, did for King was to further legitimize the new movement he was anointed to lead: If the scions of two of the most powerful and wealthy families in America supported the activism taking place, then that was all the more reason for those in the proverbial smoke-filled rooms (the politicians in Washington . . .) to take seriously the movement's demands.

Because the movement had garnered the endorsement of such powerful people, it was important for King to steer clear of Lewis Michaeux while in Harlem. Here was a man who represented everything that Malcolm X was just beginning to articulate in the same community and, within the space of five years, would popularize among young Northern Negroes as a whole: the goal of ridding oneself of all vestiges of dependency on "the goddamn white man." This was a natural outgrowth of the exhilarating atmosphere of liberation, the equivalent of marking your territory, defining for yourself who you are. Nevertheless, for King to be associated with a man like Michaeux, who articulated a position that many Caucasians considered racism in reverse, could have killed the newborn movement before it even walked.

On another front stood Izola Curry, who represented the extreme extent to which a person could take rational fears until they turned into mental illness. Curry was a complex mixture of human pride gone berserk, believing that Negroes shouldn't have to protest for rights that were naturally theirs, and that Communists had quite a bit of covert influence within civil rights organizations. In that regard she shared some of the beliefs of the leadership of the very organization she despised. Roy Wilkins and Thurgood Marshall also believed that actively protesting for rights was the wrong road for Negroes to travel down. Yet the NAACP felt compelled to support King and the Montgomery protest, both to try to appear on top of any racial confrontation taking place anywhere in the nation and because after the protest reached the courts, it entered the purview of the organization's strongest division: its legal defense fund.

Where Curry parted company with the NAACP was not only in her paranoia that the NAACP itself was controlled by Communists but in her conviction that Negroes should appeal directly to the federal government rather than to the courts for their rights. Then there was her skepticism regarding Negro preachers. Behind closed doors, plenty of fellow Negroes complained that this segment of Negro America was composed of selfish men with gigantic egos who had no other avenue for the expression of their licentiousness and greed. (Ella Baker, the first executive director of SCLC, hired until a permanent director could be found, also had her doubts about Negro preachers; it took much convincing to get her to take the job.) Did not the charges of infidelity against Abernathy, precipitating the embarrassing attack in Montgomery, and the egos King dealt with among his fellow preachers prove that these concerns were indeed merited?

After Curry stabbed King, Averell Harriman dramatized the degree to which politicians tend to say what they think voters want to hear rather than what they really believe. Then he demonstrated that for the politician the first thing that comes to mind is how it will affect the election. So he searched for a competitive advantage. Just before the crisis, through his speeches Harriman professed a belief in racial equality. Yet after it, in fearing that it was a mistake to take King to Harlem Hospital, Harriman revealed that he really didn't trust the intelligence of Negroes as he did Caucasians, even in the face of the stereotype that stabbings and shootings were all that Harlem Hospital surgeons handled. (This stood in stark contrast to the attitude of Roy Wilkins that because the hospital handled so many cases of this kind, there was nothing to worry about.) Nevertheless, Harriman rushed to Harlem Hospital to convey an electoral image of touching concern for King (a concern that no doubt, at a certain level, was sincere).

Then there were Aubré Maynard's fabrications of what happened to Martin Luther King, Jr., in the operating room. They would survive, even in King's own account of what happened. In 1998, *The Autobiography of Martin Luther King, Jr.* was published by Warner Books. In Chapter 12 entitled, "Brush with Death," King describes how he was attacked by Curry. Before the operation even began, he writes:

> I lay in bed for hours. . . . Days later when I was well enough to talk to Dr. Aubré Maynard, chief of surgeons, who performed the delicate, dangerous operation, I learned the reason for the long delay that preceded surgery. He told me that the razor tip of the instrument had been touching my aorta and that my whole chest had to be opened to extract it . . . It came out in The New York Times the next morning that if I had sneezed, I would have died.

King went on to describe how his days of convalescence in New York after the attack reinforced his conviction that the new civil rights movement had to hold on to the spirit of nonviolence. With that in mind he returned to Montgomery and got back to work. Apparently he was never told that the real reason for the delay was because Maynard could not be found. And as the preceding pages demonstrated, it had hardly been necessary to open his entire chest for an operation in which Maynard was not the principal surgeon.

The earliest known version of the truth of what happened in the operating room was revealed after publication of a short article in *The New York Times* on January 14, 1996. The occasion was King's birthday holiday. Reporter Sarah Kershaw interviewed the then ninety-four-year-old retired Maynard about the King stabbing incident and subsequent surgery. Maynard told Kershaw about being in the Plaza Theater in midtown Manhattan when King was brought in. He told her about the anger of Governor Harriman that it took so long for him to be located, and that after reassuring the governor he introduced himself to the prostrate King, then examined and reassured him. Then he told Kershaw that he immediately decided upon the manner in which King should be treated. After that, stated Maynard, "We started the surgery and it was carried out, I would say successfully." But that was as much detail as he gave. After that Maynard went on to describe the surprise of one of King's entourage the next day upon their arrival, that a "big white surgeon" had not been the one who performed the operation. Maynard concluded his account of the events to Kershaw by noting that Harlem Hospital was looked down upon, thus, "It was up to me to show the world that [we could save King]."

Two and a half weeks later John Cordice decided to break his silence regarding the details of what happened in the operating room. He wrote a letter to the *Times* acknowledging his silence over the years out of deference to Maynard. Then he went on to detail why he was breaking his silence. He stated that he wanted "serious historians" to know what really happened, and that it was also because all the other surgeons involved in the drama other than Maynard were now dead (Emil Naclerio died in 1984 of congestive heart failure at the age of sixty-nine). Finally, in addition it was because it was quite possible that he, Cordice, was suffering from prostate cancer and his own days were numbered (Cordice would survive). Then he gave his account of what really happened. But the *Times* never published the letter, probably because in Kershaw's article not enough detail of what took place was provided to merit refutation of anything Maynard said, and the details of the operation provided by Cordice ran far longer than letters in the *Times* usually run.

John Parker confirms Cordice's account of what happened that day in the operating room, saying that Naclerio told him the same thing. Another surgeon confirms Cordice's account as well. "The ones who performed all the surgery on King were Naclerio and Cordice," says Dr. Van Bockstaele, a French-born heart surgeon at Harlem Hospital.

Bockstaele, who arrived at the hospital in the early sixties, goes on to describe the relationship between Maynard and Cordice as one that was the equivalent of father and son, implying that there was some admiration and resentment on the part of both. (In fact, in 1966 when Maynard was ready to retire as Chairman of the Department of Surgery, he would ask Cordice to take over the position; Cordice turned it down, citing a distaste for the administrative duties that came with the position.)

"Cordice was extremely good," recalls Bockstaele. "But the word has to be used carefully. . . . Maynard was Machiavellian in general. And Cordice was, I won't say pure, but he couldn't understand such behavior. Cordice was the type of man who would have avoided killing a roach. Maynard, by contrast, was in a war for respect as a surgeon from the beginning of his career to the very end."

Bockstaele agrees that though Maynard was the chief of surgery, he didn't have the best surgical hands. He wasn't as skillful in the operating room as Cordice and Naclerio were. And like Cordice, Maynard originally wanted to be something it would have been impossible for a Negro in his day and age to become: an engineer. Obviously, to Maynard the next best career was being a surgeon.

He also became a Francophone. Just before becoming chief of surgery, Aubré Maynard boned up on his French and traveled to France (where he eventually met and married a frenchwoman). He got to know eminent French cardiac and pancreatic surgeons. After becoming chairman of the department, he began inviting them to lecture and demonstrate at Harlem Hospital. Because he was able to communicate with the French people in a manner that the typical American could not, his French friends looked upon him as a man, not a Negro man. Maynard appreciated that. Thus he was constantly trying to make his image more continental. In Bockstaele's opinion, one of the reasons for this was because when he came to the United States from Barbados as a teenager, Maynard was shocked by the level and degree of racism. He had trouble with many Afro-Americans because he was interested in becoming worldly and international, moving away from "blackness," so to speak. Hence his rough and bitter personality and his determination to prove him-self. And, as speculated earlier, the reason behind his exaggeration of the role he played in saving Martin Luther King, Jr.

Which provides an interesting parallel. In their early years, both Cordice and Maynard had been shielded from the worst man-ifestations of Jim Crow, only to be shocked as teenagers by what they confronted. Yet Maynard, eighteen years Cordice's senior, was more determined to prove himself in an extroverted manner. Perhaps this had everything to do with the fact that while as a young boy Cordice was shielded from Jim Crow's worst manifestations in the Deep South, still, he knew that Caucasians were ultimately in power. By contrast, though Maynard spent his early years in Barbados, which was a British colony, day-to-day it was run pri-marily by non-Caucasians and had no Jim Crow and little dis-crimination based on skin color. All the discrimination he witnessed was based on class. Thus what he confronted in the U.S. was far more shocking, even though both he and Cordice faced these realities as teenagers in New York City, where racial dis-crimination was far less potent than in the Deep South. In addition Maynard trained in medicine in a different era than Cordice, the era when specialization was just developing. Hence all the more reason for Maynard to be insecure as the years passed.

And as the years went by, the fate of the other key operatives in that traumatic week of crisis for Martin Luther King, Jr., were as follows: After losing the 1958 gubernatorial election, Averell Harriman returned to private life until the election of John F. Kennedy as pres-ident two years later. Under Kennedy he would become Assistant

Secretary of State for Far Eastern Affairs; then Undersecretary for Political Affairs and chief negotiator for the nuclear test ban treaty with the Soviet Union. In subsequent administrations (1968 and 1969), he would take part in the Paris peace negotiations relative to the Vietnam War. And in the following years he would speak out for nuclear disarmament. Averell Harriman died in 1986.

As for Nelson Rockefeller, he served as governor of New York for four successive terms, initiating a series of innovative and expensive government programs to benefit all New Yorkers culturally and economically. Rockefeller would go on to become the quintessential liberal Republican (the type of politician virtually run out of the party by 1980), causing all Republicans with views similar to his to be known as "Rockefeller Republicans." The biggest blow to his reputation, though, would come during the horrible Attica prison riot of 1971. Rockefeller ordered that the rebellion be crushed by force, killing thirty-seven men, nine hostages, and twenty-eight prisoners. Had he not ended the riot in such a shockingly brutal manner, it's possible that Nelson Rockefeller would have realized his dream of becoming president of the United States, the office he ran for in subsequent years, never making it past the Republican primaries. The closest he would come to realizing this dream was when he was chosen in 1974 as vice president by the new president of the United States, Gerald Ford, upon the resignation of President Richard Nixon due to the Watergate scandal. After stepping down upon the election of Democrat Jimmy Carter as president, Rockefeller returned to private life. He died of a heart attack in 1979.

The controversial Lewis Micheaux who, unlike Aubré Maynard, eagerly indulged his black Africanness, would go on to further prosperity for many years after his protest of King's actions. Eventually his bookstore would be said to gross over $1,500 per day, with an inventory of over a quarter of a million books about people of black African descent around the world. Michaeux would also open a branch in Hamilton, Bermuda. By 1969, he would be said to ship out ten thousand books per week to small bookstores and colleges around the country. Yet the following year he received an eviction notice compliments of one of the gubernatorial candidates who spoke at the 1958 rally he had protested. On the site where his bookstore was located, Governor Rockefeller's administration intended to construct a seventeen-story state office building, one of the many mammoth building projects it spent state money on while he was governor, and a building that would be named for Adam Clayton Powell, Jr. This facility would replace the Hotel Teresa (which by then was no longer a hotel) as the tallest structure on the Harlem skyline. After his eviction, Michaeux's bookstore was moved to a spot on the corner of 125th Street and Lenox Avenue. Lewis Micheaux would live into his nineties, dying at the age of ninety-two in 1976, celebrated as a virtual statesman at a funeral attended by numerous dignitaries.

As mentioned earlier, Emil Naclerio died of congestive heart failure in 1984 at the age of sixty-nine. Aubré Maynard, by contrast, would live to be almost one hundred. He died on March 20, 1999, at the age of ninety-seven. Upon his death there was barely a ripple at Harlem Hospital due to the fact that he was so disliked.

The following day, *The New York Times* featured a prominent obituary again claiming that Maynard had saved King. There would be no formal funeral. But there would be a memorial service two months later at Harlem Hospital. And it took some doing to get the hospital to do even that, not only because Maynard had been so disliked but because he hadn't been a real presence at the hospital for thirty-two years. Dr. Gene Ann Polk organized the affair, which took place in the Herbert G. Cave Auditorium of the hospital. And interestingly, rather than saying that Maynard had saved King, the memorial service obituary would state that Maynard was "credited" with saving King. Only about fifty people attended, including the elderly daughters of Louis T. Wright (Barbara and Jane), who had careers as physicians themselves. During the service, conspicuous for her presence was a Ms. Helen Gee, a nurse who once worked for Maynard. Gee described a kind deed performed by Maynard. She married her Chinese husband during the height of World War II when prejudice against Asians was extremely high. As a result, she could find no one to serve as witness to the marriage—except for Aubré de Lambert Maynard.

Others who spoke included Dr. Bockstaele and Dr. John Parker. Prominent among those absent from the service would be John Cordice, who retired from the practice of thoracic surgery in 1994 and is still alive today. Cordice was just one of the many who couldn't bring himself to attend due to so many mixed feelings about interactions with Maynard. Maynard's remains were cremated, after which his widow (with whom he had no children) returned to live in France.

NOTES

ONE: where do we go from here?

p. 1–14 All information on Montgomery Boycott victory and aftermath for King: *Bearing the Cross*, by David Garrow (Quill William Morrow, 1999), pp. 11–109; *Parting the Waters: America in the King Years*, by Taylor Branch (Simon and Schuster, 1988) pp. 128–271; *Stride Toward Freedom: The Montgomery Story*, by Martin Luther King, Jr., (Ballantine Books edition, 1960), pp. 11–181.

p. 2 1921 Montgomery statute prohibiting protests without just cause: Branch, *Parting the Waters, op. cit.* p. 168.

p. 9 "To prepare and preach sermons is to use up creative energy . . . ," *ibid.* p. 226.

p. 10 *Stride Toward Freedom* not needing chapter on Negro self-improvement: Garrow, *Bearing the Cross, op. cit.*, p. 105.

pp. 10–13 Quotes from "Stride Toward Freedom": *Stride Toward Freedom: The Montgomery Story*, by Martin Luther King, Jr., (Ballantine Books edition, 1960), pp. 12, 35, 109, 116, 180.

p. 13 Levison and Rustin leaving names out of credits for *Stride Toward Freedom*: Bayard Rustin: Troubles I've Seen, by Jervis Anderson, (HarperCollins, 1997), p. 210.

TWO: a tight race

p. 15 Background of Harriman and Rockefeller families: "A Voter's Choice of Millionaires," by Theodore White, *Life* magazine, September 22, 1958.

p. 16 Rockefeller's career accomplishments up to 1958: "Why You Should Vote for Rockefeller" campaign handout, located in Averell Harriman Collection, manuscript division at Library of Congress, Washington, D.C.

p. 17 Harriman's career accomplishments up to 1958: "Advances Under the First Harriman Administration" campaign handout, located in Averill Harriman Collection, manuscript division at Library of Congress, Washington, D.C.

p. 19 Competition for power between Harriman and De Sapio during Democratic gubernatorial primary in New York: *Rockefeller; The Life of Nelson A. Rockefeller*, by Cary Reich, (Doubleday, 1996) pp. 727–769.

p. 21 Harriman,s campaign literature in Negro communities featuring Daisy Bates: Harriman campaign pamphlet entitled „Leaving Prejudice Behind," located in Averell Harriman Collection, manuscript division at Library of Congress, Washington, D.C.

p. 22 "Republican officials have been counseling Negroes to be patient . . . ": *ibid.*, p. 12.

p. 23 King appearing on *The Today Show*: Branch, *Parting the Waters, op. cit.* p. 243.

p. 23 Harriman and Rockefeller's third appearance in Harlem that week: From campaign press releases located in Averell Harriman Collection, manuscript division at Library of Congress, Washington, D.C.

THREE: **putting the right spin on a huge embarassment**

p. 25 Autographed copies of "Stride" sent to Eisenhower, Nixon, etc.: Branch, *Parting the Waters, op. cit.* p. 243.

p. 26 King told he would have to be prepared to make physical sacrifices: *ibid.*, p. 237.

p. 26 King receiving correspondence about interest of journalists and writers from Japan and Sweden in meeting with him: in letters addressed to King from Henry Moon, director of Public Relations for the NAACP, dated January 28 and June 3, 1958, contained in NAACP Collection, manuscript division at Library of Congress, Washington, D.C.

p. 26 Suggested new Jim Crow targets in Montgomery: Branch, *Parting the Waters, op. cit.* p. 237.

p. 26 Alleged Abernathy infidelity incident and arrest of King: *ibid.* pp. 237–242.

p. 28 Wilkins, telegram to President Eisenhower about King arrest, and reply of Eisenhower's office through aide: Western Union telegram to Eisenhower from Wilkins, dated September 4, 1958; letter to Roy Wilkins from Rocco C. Siciliano, Special Assistant to President Eisenhower, dated September 6, 1958, both contained in NAACP Collection, manuscript division at Library of Congress, Washington, D.C.

p. 29 Reply of Harriman to King arrest in Abernathy controversy: "Excerpts from Remarks by Governor Harriman at a Rally Sponsored by the Youth March on Integrated Schools," September 19, 1958, located in Averell Harriman Collection, manuscript division at Library of Congress, Washington, D.C.

FOUR: **taking the kid glove approach**

p. 32–33 Rift between NAACP and King's SCLC: Branch, *Parting the Waters, op. cit.* pp. 186–187, 228; *Montgomery Advertiser*, November 28, 1957; *Amsterdam News*, June 1, 1957; *Tampa Daily Times*, January 8, 1958.

p. 33 Thurgood Marshall as FBI informant: *The Washington Post*, December 3, 1996.

p. 34 All information on Arthur Spingarn: Interview with Arthur Spingarn, contained in Oral History Collection at Columbia University, New York, NY.

p. 37 Eisenhower's reply to Spingarn regarding civil rights favor: Interview with Arthur Spingarn, contained in Oral History Collection at Columbia University, New York, NY.

FIVE: why isn't king signing books at my bookstore?

p. 40 All information on background of Lewis Michaeux: *The Crisis Magazine*, October 1981; *The Western Sunrise*, (undated); *Third World* (a publication of the Student Nonviolent Coordinating Committee), a series of interviews with Michaeux in five parts, conducted in 1972; *Amsterdam News*, September 4, 1976.

p. 45 Micheaux picketing King at political rally: *The Daily News*, September 21, 1958; *The New York Herald Tribune*, September 21, 1958; *Amsterdam News*, September 27, 1958.

SIX: not quite in touch with reality

p. 49 Background of Izola Curry: *The Daily News*, September 21, 1958; *The New York Herald Tribune*, September 21, 1958; *Amsterdam News*, September 27, 1958.

SEVEN: stride toward critical acclaim

p. 54 *New York Herald Tribune* book review on "Stride Toward Freedom" and articles about civil rights: *The New York Herald Tribune*, September 17, 1958.

p. 56 King's Harlem appearances prior to political rally: *Amsterdam News*, September 20, 1958.

p. 59 All details of political rally and speeches: *The New York Herald Tribune*, September 20, 1958, September 21, 1958; *Amsterdam News*, September 27, 1958.

EIGHT: crisis

p. 65–68 Details surrounding King's stabbing and being taken to Harlem Hospital: *The Daily News*, September 21, 1958; *The New York Herald Tribune*, September 21, 1958; *The Amsterdam News*, September 27, 1958.

NINE: why did they take king to harlem hospital?

p. 69–72 Charles Felton's background and whereabouts on day King came to Harlem Hospital: interview with Dr. Charles Felton, New York City, September 21, 2000.

p. 70–71 Statistics on Harlem Hospital in the 1950s: *Amsterdam News*, July 16, 1955.

p. 71 Founding of Harlem Hospital: *Surgeons to the Poor*, by Aubré Maynard, (Appleton-Century-Crofts, 1978) p. 16.

p. 71 Integration of medical staff: *ibid.* pp. 20–21.

p. 71 Most departments run by Caucasians: interview with Dr. Charles Felton, September 21, 2000.

p. 71 Large number of foreign trainees: interview with Dr. Charles Felton, September 21, 2000; Maynard, *Surgeons to the Poor, op. cit.*, p. 195.

p. 72 Harriman's whereabouts at time of stabbing: *The New York Times*, September 21, 1958; *The New York Herald Tribune*, September 21, 1958.

p. 73 Rockefeller's whereabouts after rally and on day of the stabbing: *The New York Herald Tribune*, September 20, 1958, September 21, 1958.

p. 73 Maynard at movie theater when King brought in: Maynard, *Surgeons to the Poor*, *op. cit.*, p. 184.

TEN: waiting for little napoleon

p. 76 Mount Sinai surgeons coming to Harlem Hospital to learn from trauma cases: *ibid.*, p. 105.

p. 76 Hospitals for Negro physicans to admit patients; interview with Dr. Charles Felton, New York City, September 21, 2000; interview with Dr. John Parker, Brooklyn, NY, September 13, 2000; interview with Dr. Muriel Petioni, New York City, September 6, 2000; Maynard, *Surgeons to the Poor*, *op. cit.*, p. 134.

p. 77 Typical day of Negro physician: interview with Dr. Muriel Petioni, New York City, September 6, 2000; interview with Dr. Gene Ann Polk, Englewood, New Jersey, September 12, 2000.

p. 78 Felton's memories of proper protocol around Maynard: interview with Dr. Charles Felton, New York City, September 21, 2000.

p. 79–80 Maynard's early background: Maynard, *Surgeons to the Poor*, *op. cit.*, pp. 26–39.

p. 79–80 Naclerio preparing for wedding: interview with Dr. John Cordice, New York City, November 14, 2000; *New York Post*, January 20, 1997.

p. 81 Cordice's whereabouts on day of stabbing: interview with Dr. John Cordice, New York City, November 14, 2000.

p. 82 Waiting room filling up with surgeons from other hospitals: interview with Dr. John Cordice, New York City, November 14, 2000; Maynard, *Surgeons to the Poor*, *op. cit.*, p. 185.

p. 82 Initial operating room procedure on King: interview with Dr. John Parker, Brooklyn, NY, September 13, 2000; interview with Dr. Van Bochstaele, New York, City, November 10, 2000.

ELEVEN: roots

p. 83–88 All of Cordice's background: interviews with Dr. John Cordice, New York City, November 14, 2000, February 6, 2001.

p. 88–89 John Parker's Martha's Vineyard encounter with Maynard: interview with Dr. John Parker, Brooklyn, NY, September 13, 2000.

p. 89–93 Background of Dr. Louis T. Wright: *Journal of the National Medical Association*, March 1953; *Contemporary Black Biography*, vol. 4, edited by Barbara C. Bigelow, (Gale Research, Inc., 1993) p. 283; Maynard, *Surgeons to the Poor*, *op. cit.*, p. 96.

p. 91 Maynard's two-year houseship and obtaining junior staff position after training: Maynard, *Surgeons to the Poor*, *op. cit.*, pp. 53–54.

p. 91 Wright scoring higher than all but one other: *Journal of the National Medical Association*, March 1953.

p. 92 Wright deciding who could join staff at Harlem Hospital: interview with Dr. John Cordice, New York City, November 14, 2000; interview with Dr. John

Parker, Brooklyn, NY, September 13, 2000; Maynard, *Surgeons to the Poor, op. cit.*, p. 53.

p. 92   The 1932 controversy at Harlem Hospital: *Amsterdam News*, various issues, November 1932 to April 1933; Maynard, *Surgeons to the Poor, op. cit.*, pp. 97–98.

p. 93–96   Cordice's efforts to become a surgical resident at Harlem Hospital: interview with Dr. John Cordice, New York City, November 14, 2000.

p. 98   Wright allegedly recommending Maynard as his successor if he should die suddenly and Maynard appointed over objections of Harlem Hospital board: Maynard, *Surgeons to the Poor, op. cit.*, pp. 162–165.

p. 99   Cordice research paper controversy: interview with Dr. John Cordice, New York City, November 14, 2000.

p. 99   Naclerio background; *New York Post*, January 20, 1997; Maynard, *Surgeons to the Poor, op. cit.*, pp. 142–143.

p. 99   Dr. Helen Mayer background: Maynard, *Surgeons to the Poor, op. cit.*, pp. 140–141.

p. 100   Maynard's inability to improvise in the operating room, etc.: interviews with Dr. John Cordice, New York City, November 14, 2000, February 6, 2001; interview with Dr. Van Bochstaele, New York City, November 10, 2000.

p. 101   Attending Surgeons not wanting to scrub with Chief Resident John Parker: interview with Dr. John Parker, Brooklyn, NY, September 13, 2000.

p. 101–102   Further training for Cordice in thoracic surgery: interview with Dr. John Cordice, New York City, November 14, 2000; Maynard, *Surgeons to the Poor, op. cit.*, p. 158.

p. 103   Cordice's problems with Maynard: interviews with Dr. John Cordice, New York City, November 14, 2000, February 6, 2001.

TWELVE: saving king

p. 105   Southern racists sending Curry money: *Amsterdam News*, October 4, 1958.

p. 105   Curry's fate after the stabbing: *The Daily News*, September 21, 1958; *The New York Herald Tribune*, September 21, 1958; *Amsterdam News*, September 27, 1958; October 11, 1958.

p. 106   Maynard leaving the theater and heading to Manhattan General then Harlem Hospital to treat King: Maynard, *Surgeons to the Poor, op. cit.*, pp. 184–185.

p. 107–108   Description of what Maynard found upon arriving at Harlem Hospital, including Governor's annoyance: *ibid.*, pp. 185–187; *The New York Times*, January 14, 1996.

p. 108–110   Precise description of what happened in the operating room: interviews with Dr. John Cordice, New York City, November 14, 2000, February 6, 2001; letter from Dr. Cordice to *The New York Times*, dated January 31, 1996.

p. 110–112   Maynard's version of what happened: *The Daily News*, September 21, 1958; *Amsterdam News*, September 27, 1958; Maynard, *Surgeons to the Poor, op. cit.*, pp. 188–190.

p. 111–112 Counter arguments to Maynard's version of the operation: interview with Dr. John Cordice, New York City, November 14, 2000; February 6, 2001; letter from Dr. Cordice to The New York Times, January 31, 1996.

p. 111 The "Cluster of Pemrose drains" and Dr. Wylie allegedly being impressed with it: Maynard, *Surgeons to the Poor, op. cit.*, pp. 189–191.

p. 111–112 King's discharge on 14th postoperative day: *ibid.* p. 191.

THIRTEEN: convalescence

p. 113 King's family at the hospital: *Amsterdam News*, September 27, 1958, October 4, 1958.

p. 114 Harriman returning to hospital: *ibid.*, October 4, 1958.

p. 114 Curry's fate after the stabbing: *The Daily News*, September 21, 1958; *The New York Herald Tribune*, September 21, 1958; *Amsterdam News*, September 27, 1958, October 4, 1958, October 11, 1958.

p. 116 Wilkins, reaction to the stabbing: *The New York Times*, September 21, 1958; letter to King dated September 25, 1958, contained in NAACP Collection, manuscript division at Library of Congress, Washington, D.C.

p. 116 King's press conference during convelescence: *Amsterdam News*, October 4, 1958.

p. 116 King's release from hospital: *Amsterdam News*, October 11, 1958.

p. 117 Truman's press release denying support of Rockefeller: located in Averell Harriman Collection, manuscript division at Library of Congress, Washington, D.C.

p. 117–118 Adam Clayton Powell's behavior during gubernatorial election, Rockefeller gala, and Negro vote during election: *Rockefeller; The Life of Nelson A. Rockefeller*, by Cary Reich, (Doubleday, 1996), pp. 755–757.

FOURTEEN: subsequent fates

p. 119 One third of housestaffs being foreign graduates by 1960, 48% in NYC hospitals: *ibid.*, p. 194.

p. 120 Twenty-three Harlem Hospital housestaff failing foriegn medical exams: *ibid.*, p. 196.

p. 120–121 Recommendation of affilation between Columbia and Harlem Hospital and the controversy it caused: interviews with Dr. Felton; Maynard, *Surgeons to the Poor, op. cit.*, pp. 202–212.

p. 121 Weakness of the Department of Internal Medicine and the controversy involved: interview with Dr. Charles Felton, New York City, September 21, 2000.

epilogue

p. 125 King's misstatement of facts regarding surgery: *The Autobiography of Martin Luther King, Jr.*, edited by Clayborne Carson, (Warner Books, 1998), pp. 117–120.

p. 127 Parker and Bochstael's confirmation of Cordice's accounts of surgery and Maynard: interview with Dr. John Parker, Brooklyn, NY, September 13, 2000.